Painting AMERICANA

JUDY MORGAN, CDA

NORTH LIGHT BOOKS
CINCINNATI, OHIO
www.artistsnetwork.com

Published by North Light Books, an imprint of F&W Publications, Inc., 4700 E. Galbraith Rd., Cincinnati, Ohio 45236. (800) 289-0963. First edition.

Other fine North Light Books are available from your local bookstore, art supply store or directly from the publisher.

08 07 06 05 04   5 4 3 2 1

Library of Congress Cataloging-in-Publication Data

Morgan, Judy
  Painting Americana / Judy Morgan.
    p. cm.
  Includes index.
  ISBN 1-58180-509-8
  1. Tole painting. 2. Folk art. I. Title.

TT385.M66 2004
745.7'23--dc22   20040443363

Edited by Kathy Kipp

Designed by Marissa Bowers

Page Layout by Karla Baker

Production coordinated by Kristen Heller

Photographed by Tim Grondin

Photo styling by Nora Martini

Photographs on pages 40, 50, 72, 84, 94 and 116 shot on location at The Hatfield Inn, Lebanon, Ohio, 513-932-3193.

About the Author

Judy Morgan, CDA, is a popular painter and designer who owns her own business called Apple Cheeks Publications. She has designed over 90 pattern packets and has self-published two project books. Judy has published in *Decorative Artist's Workbook*, *The Decorative Painter*, *Tole World*, *Artist's Journal* and *Painting* magazines. She received her CDA certification from the Society of Decorative Painters in 1990 and teaches classes and seminars from coast to coast. Her designs can be seen on her Web site: www.applecheeks.net.

METRIC CONVERSION CHART

TO CONVERT	TO	MULTIPLY BY
Inches	Centimeters	2.54
Centimeters	Inches	0.4
Feet	Centimeters	30.5
Centimeters	Feet	0.03
Yards	Meters	0.9
Meters	Yards	1.1
Sq. Inches	Sq. Centimeters	6.45
Sq. Centimeters	Sq. Inches	0.16
Sq. Feet	Sq. Meters	0.09
Sq. Meters	Sq. Feet	10.8
Sq. Yards	Sq. Meters	0.8
Sq. Meters	Sq. Yards	1.2
Pounds	Kilograms	0.45
Kilograms	Pounds	2.2
Ounces	Grams	28.3
Grams	Ounces	0.035

Acknowledgments

So many people come to mind when I think of all the encouragement and support I have had over the years, and the new friends I have made at North Light Books while writing this book.

Thank you to my regular weekly class, who have become more friends than students; I look forward to seeing them every Wednesday.

I would like to acknowledge Jo Sonja Jansen who has been an inspiration to me for the last fifteen years. The highlight of my year is her Design and Composition seminar.

A special thank you to Sechtem's Wood Products and Unique Woods. They are always there for me when I need something special made up and so generous with their products.

Also thank you to Rosemary Reynolds of DecoArt, Barbara Carson of Delta Technical Coatings, Lois Kline at Chroma Inc., and Loew-Cornell, for your wonderful paints and brushes.

And I must not forget to mention the Society of Decorative Painters (SDP); without this organization I would not be where I am today.

A very special thanks to the wonderful people at North Light Books who made this experience so rewarding. I would like to mention a few people in particular: Maureen Berger who was exceptional to work with, thank you so much for your help and support. Kathy Kipp, who was the first person I met at North Light—thanks for picking me out of the mass of creative painters out there. And to all the other people at North Light who made me feel so welcome there.

Dedication

This book is dedicated to my faithful and supportive husband Dennis, and daughters Laina and Krista who grew up with a stay-at-home artist/mom and suffered the consequences. My husband Dennis never complains when I am off for weeks at a time doing something that involves painting, be it seminars or conventions. He also doesn't complain about the many soup-and-grilled-cheese dinners over all these many years.

I'd also like to mention my painting friend, Caroline Bose, CDA. She has been helping me with every trade show since the beginning in 1996. We've had way too much fun!

Table of Contents

Introduction

Often I am asked to explain exactly what "decorative art" is. Sometimes it is called "tole painting." Tole, however, refers specifically to utilitarian metal pieces that have been adorned with paint; but of course, many other types of surfaces may be decoratively painted. (I try not to laugh too hard when someone who has heard that I am a tole painter asks if I paint on "toes"— as in "toe painter.")

"Folk art" is another term often applied to decorative painting, but that, too, limits the definition because not all decorative painting is done in the primitive or "country" style usually associated with folk art. Simply put, decorative painting is the work of artists who adorn objects, utilitarian or otherwise, with paint and brush, rather than using flat surfaces such as paper and canvas. (Even this definition is somewhat limiting; this book includes a sampler project painted on a flat board.)

I was introduced to decorative painting in the early 1980s when I was creating apple dolls for the gift-store market. While attending the Gift Market in Los Angeles California, I saw many examples of decorative painting being produced for the mass market. These intrigued me, because prior to my involvement in the doll business, I had been a fine art painter. As soon as I had a chance, I began taking decorative painting lessons, and I've never looked back.

Now I cringe when someone asks me if decorative painting is a "craft." Clearly, some painters devote more time to the study of decorative art and some become more adept than others, but decorative painting is as much an art as is painting on canvas. Just as with any of the "fine" arts, the appeal and value of a finished piece are really matters of personal preference.

Decorative art is all around us, even more so than is fine art. It is on our walls in the form of wallpaper, on our furniture as fabric patterns, on our dishes and towels and even on our greeting cards. It is so much a part of our everyday lives that we tend to take it for granted, yet someone had to sit down with pencil and paper or paint and canvas to create the designs that surround us. Next time you buy a greeting card or pick up a home decorating magazine, open your eyes to the creativity and talent behind the beautiful designs you see.

Interest in decorative painting continues to grow as many people turn again to the humanity displayed in handpainted items. The fast-paced age of computers in which we live can be overwhelming, and rooms full of plain gray machines offer us little comfort at the end of the day.

It is no wonder, then, that we are gravitating toward "nesting": turning our homes into warm and inviting sanctuaries that reflect our own personalities and values.

When my editor and I met to outline this book, our goal was to provide a variety of projects, from folk landscapes to florals, that would help both beginning and advanced painters add a personal touch to the objects that surround them. If you find these projects enjoyable as well as informative, then our efforts have been worthwhile, and this decorative artist is happy.

Chapter 1

SUPPLIES

SURFACES

I like to use surfaces that are fairly easy to find and generic enough to make adaptation easy for the decorative painter. You can reduce or enlarge the designs in this book to fit your specific needs. And always keep in mind that you may have to eliminate or add an element to make a composition work. Adjust the sizes of your brushes to the size of your project.

SURFACE PREPARATION

If you are working on a wood surface you will have to seal the piece with either penetrating oil-based wood sealer, or a water-based sealer. This is a personal preference and one is just as good as the other. If you are sensitive to oil-based products use the water-based instead. The difference between the two is that oil-based sealers penetrate the wood surface and are usually shellac plus denatured alcohol, which is a solvent. And it's powerful stuff. Use it in a well-ventilated area. Water-based sealers tend to sit on the surface of the wood, so when you sand before painting, some of the dried sealer will slough off.

If you paint on metal you must prep with either metal primer, preferably sandable metal primer, or with an acrylic brush-on metal sealer. If you opt for the acrylic sealer, let the piece cure for a few weeks before painting. If you are in a hurry, choose the sandable metal primer.

No matter what the surface is, sand lightly before you basecoat. This gives the surface a "tooth": something for the paint to cling to. Use a tack cloth to remove the dust from sanding.

When you basecoat your surface you should put on as many coats of paint as you need to provide complete coverage. Four thin coats of paint are better than one thick and lumpy coat of paint.

TRACING THE PATTERN

Always trace your pattern on tracing paper or vellum. Don't skip this step. You may need to reapply some details at a later time and it is very difficult to see through white bond paper.

I use a permanent ink pen like a fine-point Sharpie pen to trace; that way the ink doesn't get all over my hands or smear on the paper.

The easiest way to transfer the pattern onto your surface is with graphite paper, which is available at any craft or art supply store. Carbon paper does not work well for your painting projects as it is extremely hard to remove later. In the projects in this book, I refer to light or dark graphite paper. It also comes in colors, but all you really need are light and dark. After you are finished painting, you can remove the graphite lines with a craft eraser; don't use the one on the end of your pencil.

Beginners like to trace the entire pattern, comma strokes to dots. And I understand, having once been a beginner myself. But you don't always need to trace everything. I like to trace the basic pattern lines and refer to the pattern as I paint. The more detail you transfer, the more you will have to erase later.

Place the tracing paper on the surface and tape it down in a couple of places with either blue painters tape or Scotch Magic tape; this will prevent the pattern from moving as you trace. Place either light or dark graphite paper under the tracing and transfer the pattern to your surface with a stylus.

BRUSHES

Your painting will only be as good as the brushes you use. They are your most important tools and you should take excellent care of them, as sometimes they can be expensive. For the projects in this book, I use Loew-Cornell brushes (see Resources, page 126).

Different brushes have different jobs to do. A wash brush is either a flat or a filbert shape about ¾-inch (19mm) to 1-inch (25mm) wide, and is intended for use with a lot of paint and/or water. Use it for basecoating or applying thinned coats of paint in larger areas.

A basing brush is usually a synthetic brush with white bristles, and is designed to take more abuse than other brushes.

I use a Loew-Cornell 1½-inch (38mm) Flat Sky Wash brush for varnishing as well as for laying on lots of color at one time. Because of its large size you can apply varnish quickly and evenly.

The Loew-Cornell Duster/Stippler is a specialty brush used for faux finishes. It looks like a large stencil brush, but the bristle end is rounded, not flat.

The Bringle Blender is a brush used for stippling or dry-brushing. It's available from Bette Byrd Brushes (see Resources, page 126).

A flat brush is used for basecoating or for floating/side-loading color.

A filbert brush is like a flat brush only the end of the brush is an oval shape; they make great comma strokes and base small areas nicely because the soft shape doesn't leave paint ridges.

A round brush can be used to basecoat small areas or to pull strokes.

A liner brush is for pulling thin lines of color or for outlining.

A mop brush is used for softening the edges of paint.

BRUSH CARE

Now that you have invested in all these wonderful brushes, you must care for them properly.

Always, always wet them thoroughly in water before you pick up any acrylic paint in them. Rinse them out frequently in your brush basin. The basins usually have molded ridges in the bottom for the purpose of running the brush across them to release the paint. My favorite brush basin has two water wells, one for clean water and one with ridges. The clean water side has brush rests built in where you can keep the brushes clean and handy for the next time you need them. If you are not going to use a brush anytime soon, keep it out of the water. Waterlogged brushes will not last as long.

When you are finished painting for the day, wash your brushes with soap made expressly for that purpose or use something gentle like Murphy's Oil Soap. Never use dish detergent or bath soap. The dish detergent is too drying and harsh on the delicate brush hairs. Bath soap is for skin; you wouldn't wash your hair with a bar of soap, would you?

Never use hot water to wash acrylic paint out of your brushes. Room temperature tap water is best.

Pinch the brushes into their original shape and stand them bristle side up in a protective brush case.

If you ever get an uncooperative stray hair in a brush, pull it out with a pair of tweezers; don't cut it off with scissors.

These are the basic supplies I used to paint the projects in this book. The "Colors & Materials" page in each project gives you a specific list of the paint colors, brushes, and miscellaneous items you'll need to paint that project.

Paints and Miscellaneous Supplies

PAINTS & MEDIUMS

For the projects in this book, I used Delta Ceramcoat and DecoArt Americana acrylic paints. Most art and craft supply stores carry both brands, so you shouldn't have any trouble finding them. They both have a nice creamy consistency, and the color mixes are always the same.

The list of paint mediums is endless. All are designed to assist you in achieving different effects with your painting. I have used only a few mediums for the projects in this book, such as "Crackle Medium" and "Faux Glaze Medium." "Extender" medium is a must-have in anyone's paint box. Different paint companies call this product by different names. Delta makes "Color Float," a blending medium/water conditioner, great for shading and line work. Delta also makes "Gel Blending Medium" which extends the drying time of acrylic paint. You can also try "Textile," "Glass & Tile," "Iridescents" and "Texture" mediums.

PALETTE PAPER

I use a pad of waxed palette paper made specifically for acrylic paint. I don't remove a piece of palette paper to use it, I just leave it attached to the rest of the pad. When I'm finished with it, I just tear it off and dispose of it.

There are also palette boards on the market now. You simply wash off the dried paint and reuse it. I have both, and prefer using the palette pad.

MISCELLANEOUS SUPPLIES

I like to use a soapstone pencil for adding elements and making reference points or sketching directly on my painted surface. The soapstone can be removed with water. If you cannot find a soapstone pencil at your craft store, try looking in the electrician's section of a hardware store.

I keep a white chalk pencil in my box of supplies as well. The chalk is a little more impervious to water and can be removed with an eraser.

A plastic mushroom brush can be found at cookware stores. I use it to create a faux-linen effect (see page 12).

You should always have a small 6-inch (15.2cm) ruler in your paint box. It comes in handy when you need to trace a straight line. I also like to have a 12-inch (30.5cm) T-rule handy; it helps keep designs parallel on my painting surface.

I also keep on hand a large kneaded eraser, a small pair of scissors, a compass, a sea sponge, a color wheel and paper towels.

What climate do you paint in? You are very fortunate if you are an acrylic painter and live in a somewhat humid climate.

I live in Southern California, which is semi-arid, so I have had to make some adjustments. If I am going to float color, I brush some clean water over the area, or use an extender to keep the paint from drying out too quickly. If it is particularly dry, I use a humidifier in my studio. Of course, the opposite problem is the painter who cannot get her painting to dry because she lives in Florida or Ohio. She needs to keep a small desk fan or a hair dryer handy at all times.

Finishing Supplies

After you have finished your project and the paint is dry, be sure to remove any graphite lines or pencil lines. Use an eraser or odorless brush cleaner to remove them. Apply the brush cleaner with a paper towel.

Wood surfaces can be finished with a water-based, brush-on varnish such as Delta Interior/Exterior Matte Varnish. Apply water-based varnish with a 2-inch (51mm) varnish brush, making sure not to overwork the varnish. Try to lay the varnish on with one sweeping brushstroke. Allow the varnish to dry well before applying a second coat. You can also use Delta Varnish on metal pieces as well.

If I am going to "antique" a piece, I like to first spray on Krylon Matte Finish #1311 because it leaves a "toothy" finish for the antiquing mediums to hold on to. One thing to always remember: If you have used oil products to antique a painted piece, you cannot varnish with an acrylic, it won't stick. Use a spray varnish like Blair Harvest Tole. After you finish antiquing, clean your brush thoroughly with odorless brush cleaner or Murphy's Oil Soap. See page 15 for instructions on how to antique a finished painting.

Be sure to follow the manufacturers' directions for all the products mentioned.

Shown here are light and dark graphite papers and a stylus for transferring your patterns; a plastic mushroom brush for applying a "faux linen" effect to a painted surface; a spray matte finish; and a matte exterior/interior varnish.

Chapter 2

TIPS & TECHNIQUES

FAUX-LINEN LOOK

The Shaker Sampler project on pages 40-49 begins with a board painted to look like linen. To achieve this linen look, basecoat the entire surface with Fawn. Place Fawn + Desert Sand 1:1 on your palette, and add enough water to the paint to make it the consistency of milk. Dip a plastic mushroom brush into the mix; you may have to really push the brush into the mix deeply to get enough on the brush. Comb horizontally and vertically across the board to create a hand-woven linen look. Let dry.

SLIP-SLAP

The size of the area to be slip-slapped determines the size of the brush; you can use a flat or a filbert for this technique. Apply the paint in an X pattern, pulling across the area in one direction, then the other. The brush makes a slip-slap sound as you do this.

Your paint should be on the dry side; to do this, pick up some paint in the brush, then go to a clean spot on the palette and brush back and forth until the paint starts to get a sticky feel.

You can get a dry-brush effect with this technique as well.

STIPPLING

Basecoat the surface with your base color and let dry. Dip a duster/stippler brush in water, then pinch out as much water as you can on a paper towel. Load the duster/stippler into another color and pounce the color onto your surface, holding the brush handle straight up. If you live in a dry climate, it helps to dampen the surface with water before stippling so the paint doesn't build up too quickly and look spotty.

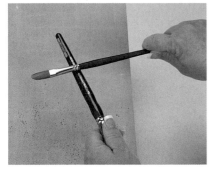
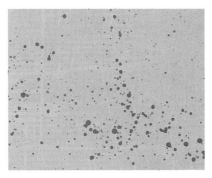

FLY-SPECKING OR SPATTERING

1 Load a large filbert brush with thinned paint (the consistency of cream). Hold another large brush, with the bristles in your hand, over the surface to be fly-specked. Tap the filbert brush on the other brush handle.

2 The size of the specks is determined by the amount of paint in the brush.

Try this over a piece of paper first to get an idea of how it works. Remember to protect your work surface from any overspray.

WET ON WET

Brush on a coat of your background color; while the paint is still very wet, pick up your second color on the same brush. Apply the paint in the same way you did the slip-slap (see page 12). The wet on wet effect is softer because you are making another value (lighter or darker) of the background.

Work most of the paint into the middle. As you work the paint out, it will get closer in value to the background. When the paint starts to get sticky and grabs, stop and let it dry. You can always go back and apply more paint later.

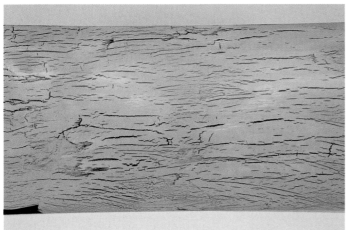

CRACKLE FINISH

1 There are several different products on the market that crackle paint; some are a one-step process, others are a two-step process. For this demonstration I used a one-step process, which usually gives you larger cracks. In most cases the background color for crackling is dark, so the cracks will show more effectively.

Basecoat the surface with enough paint to cover. Following the manufacturer's instructions, apply a generous coat of the crackle medium over the based surface. Try not to overwork the medium, as it may get sticky and grab at the brush, then start to "roll" or mound up in places, which you do not want to happen. At this point you can let it air dry or use a hair dryer to speed up the drying process.

Put on a generous coat of your final color of paint; the more paint, the bigger the cracks. Again, don't overwork the paint.

2 Let the paint air dry or put it in front of a fan. I have never had something crackle the same way twice, so don't be concerned if doesn't look exactly like this.

Flip-Float & Comma Strokes

FLIP-FLOAT

Sideload a large flat brush with the color of your choice and blend on your palette. Pull the color in a straight line (like you would normally pull a shade or highlight float), then flip the brush over and pull another float next to and slightly overlapping the first float. It is okay to go over the float a few times to blend the paint together in the middle where the two floats meet. It sometimes helps to brush water or a floating medium or extender over the surface first to keep the paint wet longer.

COMMA STROKES

You can do a comma stroke with just about any brush you have, but the best-looking comma strokes are done with either a round brush or a filbert brush. Load your brush with enough paint to complete the stroke; don't be stingy with the paint. The paint should be at least halfway up the bristles but not into the ferrule. Support your hand with your pinky finger or the side of your hand, and hold the brush at a 90-degree angle to the surface so that gravity can help the paint flow off the bristles. The most common mistake at first is holding a brush like a pencil.

To start the stroke, apply pressure to the brush so that the brush hairs are bent at almost a 90-degree angle. This deposits most of the paint at the beginning of the stroke, giving it that nice rounded "head."

Pull the brush back (pull from the elbow, not the wrist) and let off on the pressure, pulling slightly to the right or left to get the curved shape. The brush hairs will straighten and go back to a point, making the "tail" of the stroke.

Making great comma strokes takes lots of practice, but in the end, you'll be rewarded with beautiful strokes that seem to come naturally.

STRAIGHT COMMA STROKES

These are painted exactly like curved comma strokes, but instead of pulling them to the right or left, pull them straight towards you. Sometimes it helps to slightly roll the brush between your thumb and forefinger as you pull back; this helps bring the tip of the brush back to a point.

Antiquing

1 Here I'm using the "Apple Valley Clock" from Project 6 to demonstrate how I antique a surface. First, I spray the finished piece with Krylon Matte Finish. Several light coats are better than one heavy coat. Spray at room temperature in a well-ventilated area. I have found that if the room is too cold the finish might feel bumpy like an orange peel. The finish dries in about 15 minutes.

2 I then place a ring of Burnt Umber tube oil paint on my palette. I pour a small amount of Winsor & Newton Blending & Glazing Medium into the center of the ring. This keeps the medium from running off the palette.

3 Then I pour a small amount of the Blending & Glazing Medium onto a pad of paper toweling, and apply an even, light coat over the entire painted surface.

4 I take an old no. 14 flat brush and dress it in the Blending & Glazing Medium, then pinch out the excess into a paper towel. I pick up a small amount of the Burnt Umber oil paint on a corner of the brush and place the paint in the areas that I wish to darken.

5 For the clock project I place the Burnt Umber next to the border, in the shaded areas of the hills, in the pumpkin furrows, and in the "ditch" of the plate bead between the black outer-most edge and the vine-painted rim.

6 Finally I take a 1-inch (25mm) mop brush and soften the antiquing by lightly "dusting" across the oil in a criss-cross action. If you only push the oil in one direction, you will move it out of the areas you want to deepen and eventually you'll pick it all up into the mop brush. To see how the clock looks with the antiquing, turn to page 72.

WATERING CAN

Chickens and roosters continue

to be a favorite with decorative painters.

In fact, I think we will see chickens and

roosters as popular themes in home decorating

for a long time to come.

Strutting roosters were a favorite subject

of American folk artist Peter Ompir, and

I have borrowed on his simple folk style

of painting for this piece. Of course, what

Ompir piece would be complete without

lots of comma strokes?

This is a great project for the beginning

painter as all of the strokes are simple and

fun to do. The watering can is available at

any home center.

Patterns

These patterns may be hand-traced or photo-copied for personal use only. Enlarge at 125% to bring them up to full size.

Colors & Materials

Paint: Delta Ceramcoat Acrylics

Apple Green

Barn Red

Black Green

Cloudberry Tan

Dark Chocolate

Dark Victorian Teal

Empire Gold

Gamal Green

Light Foliage Green

Light Ivory

Light Victorian Teal

Mallard Green

Old Parchment

Raw Sienna

Rouge

Tangerine

Mallard Green +
Black Green 1:1

Mallard Green +
Old Parchment 1:1

Raw Sienna +
Dark Chocolate 1:1

Tangerine +
Old Parchment 1:1

Surface

- Galvanized metal watering can with brass trim, available at home or gardening centers

Brushes

- 1-inch (25mm) wash
- no. 14 flat
- no. 2 round
- no. 6 filbert
- no. 0 liner

Additional Supplies

- Light and dark graphite paper
- Stylus
- Blue painters tape
- Grey sandable metal primer

Transfer the Pattern

1 Wash the watering can in warm soapy water to remove any dust or oily residue. Rinse. Let dry for 24 hours or place in a warm oven to dry. Tape off the brass with blue painters tape. Spray with the grey metal primer, two light coats. Let dry. Remove the painters tape. Using a 1-inch (25mm) basing or wash brush, basecoat the primed areas with Dark Victorian Teal, at least two coats to cover. Let dry between coats.

2 Tape the pattern to the can with blue painters tape and slip the light graphite paper under the pattern. Trace over the pattern lines with a stylus.

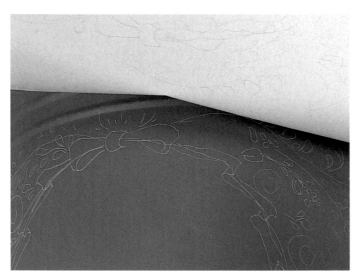

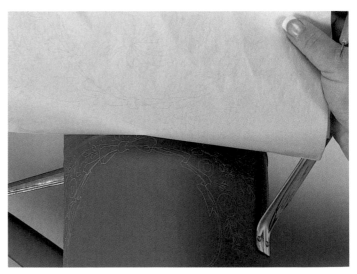

3 Use enough pressure on the stylus to make sure the white lines will show on the dark background. Lift your pattern and graphite paper to check your lines as you go.

4 At this time transfer only the background behind the rooster and the stroke pattern at the sides. The rooster will be transferred after the background has been applied.

Basecoating

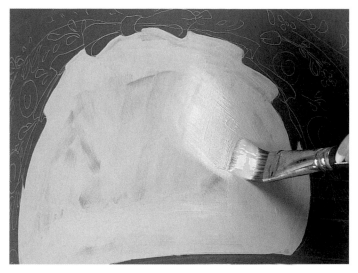

5 Load a no. 14 flat brush with Light Victorian Teal and basecoat the area behind the rooster. Use two coats to cover, letting the first coat dry completely before applying the second coat. Use a no. 2 round brush to basecoat next to the ribbon for better control.

6 After the background has dried completely, transfer the basic pattern lines of the rooster using dark graphite paper and a stylus.

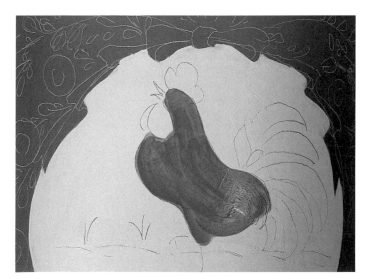

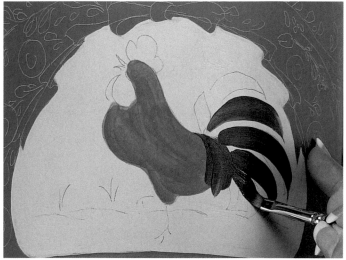

7 Use a no. 6 filbert loaded with Raw Sienna to base in the rooster's body.

8 Base the dark tail feathers and the saddle feathers with a no. 6 filbert and Dark Chocolate.

Rooster

9 Base in the light tail feathers with a no. 6 filbert and Raw Sienna.

10 Using a no. 2 round brush and Barn Red, base in the comb and wattle. Add a touch of Dark Chocolate to the Barn Red for the back wattle to make it recede a bit.

11 Using a no. 0 liner brush and Dark Chocolate, stroke in the beak. Turn the watering can upside down so you can pull the strokes toward you.

12 Turn the can upright again. Using a no. 0 liner brush and Dark Chocolate, paint a small circle for the eye.

13 Load a no. 0 liner with Dark Chocolate and paint the leg, then pull three strokes for the feet, following the pattern lines.

14 Highlight the rooster's comb and wattle with a no. 6 filbert and Rouge. This first highlight is stroked over the basecoat; keep this layer of color slightly smaller and towards the left of the comb.

15 Highlight the rooster's comb and wattle a second time with a no. 2 round brush and Tangerine. Note that each successive highlight is slightly smaller than the last. The third and final highlight is Tangerine + Light Ivory 1:1 using the no. 2 round brush.

16 Transfer the neck feather lines and the wing lines with light graphite paper and a stylus.

Rooster, continued

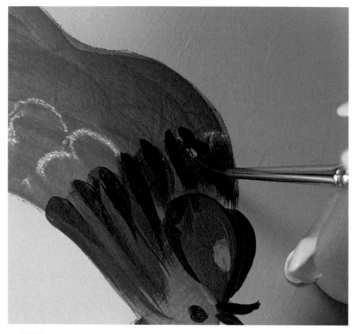

17 Turn the watering can upside down. Using a no. 2 round brush and a mix of Raw Sienna + Dark Chocolate 1:1, base in the lower neck feathers with straight comma strokes. The darkest strokes at the lower neck are Dark Chocolate applied with a no. 0 liner brush.

18 Load no. 0 liner brush with Tangerine and stroke in the middle neck feathers. Then using Old Parchment with a touch of Tangerine on a no. 0 liner, highlight the top of the head with short strokes.

19 Turn the watering can right side up again. Highlight the beak with a no. 0 liner and Raw Sienna.

20 Highlight the eye and the beak with Old Parchment using a no. 0 liner.

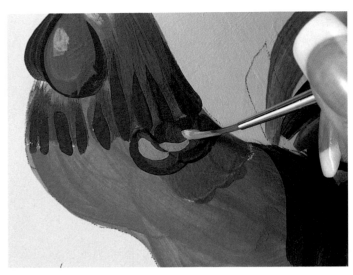

21 Using a no. 2 round brush, base in the top of the wing with Dark Chocolate. Load the same brush with Tangerine and base in the bottom of the wing.

22 Highlight the top of the wing with a no. 2 round brush and a mix of Dark Chocolate and Raw Sienna 1:1. Then using a no. 0 liner loaded with Old Parchment added to the mix above, highlight the top of the wing again. These are three progressively smaller comma strokes pulled from the front to the back.

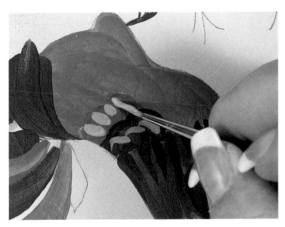

23 Turn the watering can over and using a no. 0 liner loaded with a 1:1 mix of Old Parchment and Tangerine, apply straight comma strokes across the lower wing.

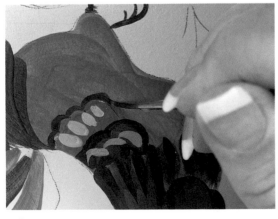

24 Load a no. 0 liner with Dark Chocolate and pull a shadow stroke under the lower wing to separate it from the body.

25 With a no. 2 round brush loaded with Empire Gold, pull dots of highlight down the front of the rooster's breast. The dots get smaller towards the legs. Thin the paint with a little water and put more dots under the wing.

Rooster's Tail Feathers

26 Use a no. 2 round brush and Tangerine thinned with water; stroke over the Raw Sienna tail feathers. Using the same brush and thinned Mallard Green, stroke over the Dark Chocolate tail feathers and the saddle feathers.

27 Turn the watering can upside down. With a no. 2 round brush and a mix of Mallard Green plus a touch of Old Parchment, make two large strokes and one smaller stroke at the base of the tail where it joins the body.

28 Load a no. 2 round brush with a mix of Mallard Green + Old Parchment 1:1, and highlight the dark tail feathers with a comma stroke pulled from the tip of the tail towards base of the tail. Keep this stroke in the middle of each tail feather.

Highlight the Raw Sienna tail feathers with a mix of Tangerine + Old Parchment 1:1, using a no. 2 round brush and keeping the stroke in the middle of the feather.

29 To accent the transition between the tail feathers and the saddle feathers, load a no. 0 liner with a mix of Mallard Green + Black Green 1:1. Pull little wiggly strokes over the gap between the tail and saddle feathers.

Foreground Foliage

30 Wet the foreground under the rooster with clean water on a no. 14 flat brush. Sideload the no. 14 flat brush with Gamal Green, blend on the palette. Pull the sideloaded strokes over the top of the foreground under the rooster. Keep this thin and transparent, letting the background show through.

31 Pick up a little Gamal Green thinned with water on a no. 6 filbert brush. Dot over the background for the bush foliage.

32 Highlight the foliage with Apple Green, using a no. 6 filbert brush. Keep the highlight towards the top of the Gamal Green dots.

33 The branches of the bushes are applied with a no. 0 liner and Dark Chocolate. Turn the watering can over and pull the strokes from the base of the bushes up.

There are also weeds in the foreground that are done in the same manner as the bush branches using the no. 0 liner and Dark Chocolate.

34 Turn the can upright and load a no. 0 liner with Light Ivory at the tip; apply a few dots of this color at the tips of the weeds.

Ribbon and Bow

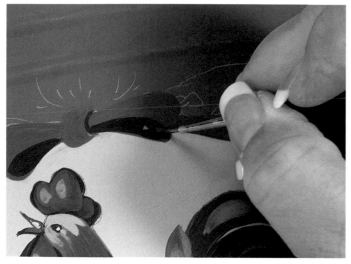

35 Load a no. 0 liner with Rouge and base in the ribbon; you'll need two coats. In the shaded areas of the ribbon, where the bow bends and where the ribbon curls, darken with Barn Red on a no. 0 liner, using two coats of paint to cover.

36 Sideload Barn Red onto a no. 14 flat brush and shade next to the knot, where the bow loops meet the ribbon, and where the ribbon bends.

Hint

When doing a "double dip" such as the Rouge + Light Ivory sideload in Step 37, always start with the base color first, in this case Rouge. Then dip into the second color before blending the two together on the palette. By dipping into the base color first, you will make it the predominant color in the blend.

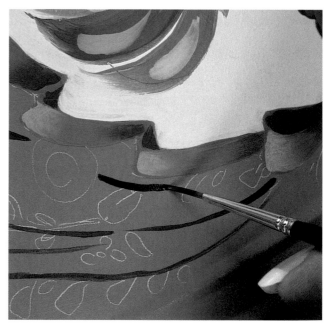

37 Sideload Rouge + Light Ivory on a no. 14 flat. Float highlights at the ends of the loops, the edges of the bends in the ribbon, and at the tips of the ribbons.

38 To base in the vines, load a no. 0 liner with Black Green, and add a little water to the brush. This will help the paint flow off the brush more easily and you will not have to load the brush as often.

Leaves and Daisies

39 Turn the can upside down and stroke in little leaves all along the vines using Black Green and a no. 0 liner.

40 Highlight the leaves with Light Foliage Green on a no. 0 liner. Remember, highlight strokes are smaller than the base strokes.

41 The second highlight on the leaves is Apple Green. Place this stroke on top of the Light Foliage Green stroke, keeping it smaller and to one side of the last stroke.

42 To begin the daisies, base a doughnut shape with Cloudberry Tan using a no. 2 round brush.

43 Base the center of each daisy with Raw Sienna. Load a no. 0 liner with Light Ivory; pull straight comma strokes from the outside into the center.

Daisies and Berries

44 Take a no. 0 liner loaded with Empire Gold and place a dot to one side of the center. The pollen dots around the center are done with a stylus dipped into Dark Chocolate; keep the dots towards the darker side of the center.

45 Tint the daisy petals with Mallard Green thinned with water; make sure the Mallard Green is very transparent. Pick up the thinned mix with a no. 2 round brush and place over the daisy petals, keeping the color towards the inside.

46 The white "dot" flowers are made by dipping the end of a brush handle into Light Ivory and placing three dots together, leaving enough space in the middle for a center dot of Raw Sienna. Re-load the brush handle for each dot to keep them the same size.

47 The red berries are created the same way using Barn Red. Dot the berries on in groups of three, but this time don't re-load the brush handle each time. This will make the berries get smaller as you dot. Let the berry dots dry. Then add a tiny dot of Rouge highlight to a few of the berries with a no. 0 liner.

Finished Watering Can

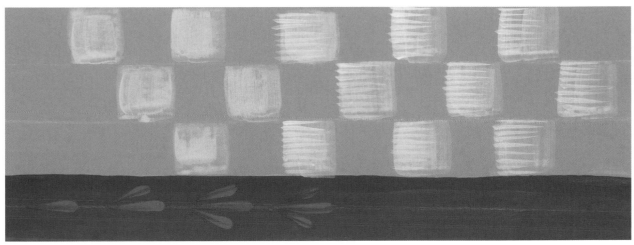

If you wish, finish the rim of the watering can with a checkerboard and strokework border. Free-hand the checks with thinned Light Ivory and let dry. Load a liner with unthinned Light Ivory and paint parallel streaks across each check. The strokework border is a series of three straight comma strokes with a dot at the base. I used Tangerine and a no. 0 liner brush. I finished off my watering can with a daisy design on the top (see the pattern for this on page 18). Use the same colors and strokes as you did for the daisies and berries surrounding the rooster. On the spout, I painted a winding vine using Black Green on a no. 0 liner.

FLORAL MIRROR

I purchased this inexpensive mirror from a local discount store. It had a wooden frame with a gold-foil finish. I liked the gold as a background for a simple garland of roses and daisies. I also used a black permanent ink pen to make the smaller designs "pop" against the background.

Before painting, I roughed up the gold foil surface with fine grit sandpaper so the acrylic paint would stick, When all painting was done, I brushed on a good water-based varnish to hold the paint down.

Look for great ready-made items like this in your local stores—they're so much fun to paint!

Pattern

This pattern may be hand-traced or photocopied for personal use only. Enlarge at 152% to bring it up to full size.

Colors & Materials

Paint: Delta Ceramcoat Acrylics

Black Green

Burnt Sienna

Coral

Empire Gold

English Yew Green

Ivory

Light Foliage Green

Old Parchment

Rhythm 'N Blue

Royal Plum

Santa's Flesh

Spice Tan

Surface

- Oval gold foil mirror from a discount store

Brushes

- no. 0 liner
- no. 2 round

Additional Supplies

- Dark graphite paper
- Stylus
- Black permanent ink pen, size .04

Vines & Leaves

1. Remove the mirror from the frame. Lightly sand the surface of the frame to give it some "tooth" and use a tack cloth to remove any sanding dust. Transfer the pattern lines with dark graphite paper and a stylus.

2. Using English Yew Green and a no. 0 liner, base in all the vines and leaves. Turn the frame as you work, and pull the vines from their tips toward the base.

3. Load a no. 0 liner with Light Foliage Green and highlight the leaves and vines.

4. Shade one side of the leaves with Black Green and a no. 0 liner.

Roses

5 Basecoat the roses with Burnt Sienna on a no. 2 round brush. One coat is all that is needed. Basecoat the center of each rose with an oval dot of Royal Plum using the same no. 2 round brush.

6 Highlight the roses with a no. 0 liner loaded with Coral tipped in Santa's Flesh; pull the back petals behind the throat of the rose first. (See the step-by-step instructions below for quick and easy stroke roses.)

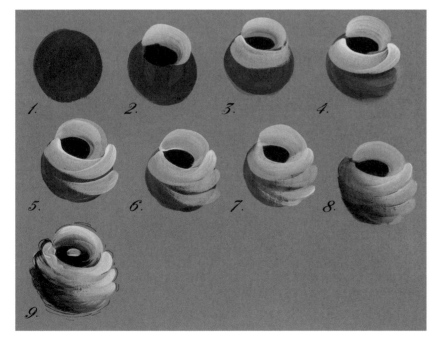

STROKE ROSES STEP BY STEP

1. Base with one coat of Burnt Sienna.

2. Paint the center with Royal Plum. The back petal is a comma stroke of Coral tipped in Santa's Flesh.

3. The front petal is painted the same way.

4. Tip the same brush into Ivory and pull a comma stroke from the right side.

5. Re-load into Coral + Santa's Flesh 1:1, blend on the palette, tip into Ivory and pull another comma stroke from the right side.

6. Pull a third comma from the right side.

7. Pull a final comma at the base.

8. Sideload a flat brush into Royal Plum and float shading on the left side of the rose.

9. Load a liner with Coral and tip into Santa's Flesh. Pull two comma strokes from the left side. Dot the center with Empire Gold. Outline the rose here and there with a black, fine-point, permanent ink pen.

Daisies

7 Base in a doughnut shape of Spice Tan for each daisy. Load a no. 0 liner with Old Parchment and pull each individual daisy petal from the outside in toward the center. Then overstroke the petals on one side of the daisy with Ivory to highlight. See the step by step instructions below for painting these little daisies.

8 When all the daisies are painted and dry, outline them here and there with a black, fine-point, permanent ink pen to make the design "pop" against the gold background.

DAISIES STEP BY STEP

1. Begin each daisy with a doughnut shape of Spice Tan.

2. Base in the center with Burnt Sienna.

3. Load a no. 0 liner with Old Parchment and pull straight comma strokes around the center for the petals. Start from the outside and pull in toward the center. Let dry.

4. Load the same brush into Ivory and place smaller highlight strokes on top of each petal. Pull a stroke of Empire Gold across the top center.

5. Dip a stylus into Black Green and place some pollen dots as shown.

6. Tint some of the daisies with Rhythm 'N Blue thinned with water. Let dry. Outline here and there with a black fine-point permanent pen.

Finished Floral Mirror

SHAKER SAMPLER

Everyone seems to love these simple schoolgirl sampler designs. A genuine antique stitched sampler can sell for more than $20,000 at the pricey auction houses.

This is another easy project for the painter who is just starting out. You can paint up a sampler like this one in no time, far faster than doing it the old fashioned way with a needle and thread. And they make wonderful gifts for friends and family, especially if you personalize them or add something like "Home Sweet Home" or "Bless this House."

I painted this design on a piece of hardboard and used a brown permanent ink pen to embellish the painting and give it a "stitched" look. The imperfect, freehand approach helps give the sampler an innocent, old-timey quality.

The frame was inexpensive, pre-finished and not at all what I wanted for the sampler. But the price was right, and I wasn't about to spend a lot of money on a custom-made picture frame. I roughed up the finish with fine sandpaper and stippled on a few colors that were used in the project, and now it looks like I did spend that extra money.

Pattern

This pattern may be hand-traced or photocopied for personal use only.
Enlarge at 208% to bring it up to full size.

Colors & Materials

Paint: DecoArt Americana Acrylics

Antique Rose

Cool White

Desert Sand

Fawn

French Grey Blue

Graphite

Hauser Light Green

Hauser Medium Green

Light Avocado

Light Mocha

Mississippi Mud

Peach Sherbet

Royal Purple

Terra Cotta

Surface

- Plywood, or gessoed hardboard available at Michaels

Brushes

- 1½-inch (38mm) varnish brush
- 1-inch (25mm) wash brush
- no. 14 flat
- no. 8 flat
- no. 2 round
- no. 0 liner
- no. 0/0 liner

Additional Supplies

- Stylus
- Dark graphite paper
- Blue painters tape
- Mushroom brush, available at cookware stores
- Brown permanent ink pen, size .01

Background

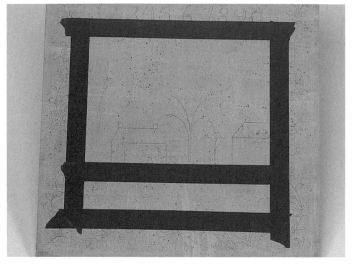

1 Basecoat the board with Fawn on a 1-inch (25mm) wash brush. To give the surface the look of linen, see "Faux-Linen Look" on page 12. To give it an antique look, fly-speck the board with Mississippi Mud (see "Fly-specking or Spattering" on page 13). Let dry. Transfer the inset lines with dark graphite paper and a stylus. Tape off the inset foreground without the pattern lines of the house and trees.

2 Sideload a 1½-inch (38mm) varnish brush with clean water. Dampen the sky area. Then sideload the brush with French Grey Blue, blend on the palette, and pull across the sky area next to the blue tape.

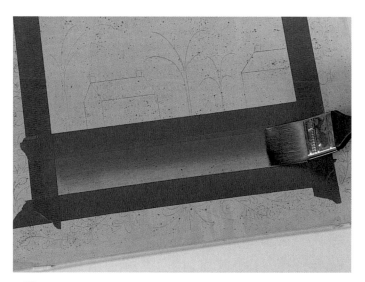

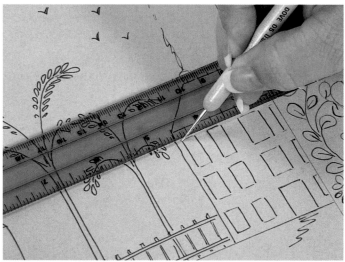

3 For the grassy area at the bottom, do the same with water, then Hauser Medium Green, sideloaded on the brush. Let dry before removing the tape.

4 Transfer all the pattern lines with dark graphite paper and a stylus.

Trees & Houses

5 Load a no. 0 liner with Mississippi Mud and base in the tree trunks and tree limbs.

6 Using a no. 0 liner brush and Hauser Medium Green, base in the leaves with straight comma strokes. The strokes at the tips of the branches are the largest. As you move down the branches toward the trunk, the leaves get smaller.

7 Base the light sides of the houses using Light Mocha. Cut in the edges with a no. 2 round, then fill in with a no. 8 flat. Three coats will be needed to cover.

Let dry between coats. Base the shady side of the left house with Desert Sand.

8 Base the roofs with Graphite. Cut in the edges with a no. 2 round, then fill in with a no. 8 flat. Let dry.

9 Transfer the architectural details such as windows, doors and chimneys with dark graphite paper and a stylus. Use a no. 8 flat and Graphite to fill in the windows. Switch to a no. 0 liner for the finer details such as the fan windows. Base the chimneys and the door on the left house with Terra Cotta. Base the door of the right house with French Grey Blue.

House Details & Sheep

10 Wet a no. 14 flat with clean water, sideload into French Grey Blue, and blend on the palette. The roof highlight is a flip-float (see page 14). After applying the float, wiggle the brush through the wet float on each side. Thin the French Grey Blue with water using a no. 2 round and add a reflection on the left side of each window.

11 Load Cool White on a no. 0/0 liner and pull a line down through the middle of the roof highlight. Pull short horizontal strokes of the same color through the vertical line of Cool White. The smoke is wiggly vertical lines of Cool White pulled up from the tops of the chimneys. Use a no. 0/0 liner and Cool White to pull a thin line across the roof eaves, then create windowpanes with the same color and brush by pulling three lines across each window and a line down the middle. Divide the fanlights with tiny lines.

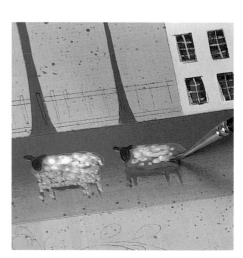

12 Mix Light Mocha and Terra Cotta 1:1; pull vertical lines on the chimneys and on the left side of the red door.

13 Basecoat the sheep with a mix of Graphite and Cool White 1:1 using a no. 2 round. Use a no. 0 liner and Graphite to paint their heads.

14 Dot in thinned Cool White over the top half of each sheep to look like fluffy wool.

Sheep, Fence & Stitching Lines

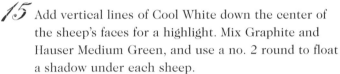

15 Add vertical lines of Cool White down the center of the sheep's faces for a highlight. Mix Graphite and Hauser Medium Green, and use a no. 2 round to float a shadow under each sheep.

16 With a no. 0 liner and Cool White, base in the fence. Create the upright pickets first, then the horizontal boards. Use thinned Mississippi Mud on a no. 0 liner and paint in a shadow next to the upright pickets and above the horizontal boards. The thinned paint is mostly water, giving it a transparent look.

17 Use a brown permanent ink pen to ink in the broken, uneven "stitching" lines around the house, tree trunks, tree leaves, birds, vines, leaves, roses and daisies.

Letters, Numbers & Border

18 LETTERS & NUMBERS

Base the letters and numbers with thinned Mississippi Mud. Base the scrolls under the numbers in the same manner.

Shade the right side of the letters and numbers with a mix of Mississippi Mud and Graphite using a no. 0 liner. This is done by pulling a shadow line following the shape of the letter or number.

When the letters and numbers are dry, pull "stitching" lines horizontally across the left side of each with the brown permanent ink pen.

19 BOW

Base the bow with French Grey Blue using a no. 0 liner brush.

Highlight the bow by adding a touch of Cool White to the French Grey Blue. Use a no. 0 liner and pull two small strokes across the knot, on each loop of the bow, and over the tails of the bow.

Shade the bow by sideloading a no. 14 flat with thinned Royal Purple and floating next to the knot on the loops and tails. Add an extra shadow with thinned Mississippi Mud on a no. 2 round. Pull this thinned color next to the tails on the right side, and under the top loop. When dry, add broken "stitching" lines with the brown permanent ink pen.

20 ROSES

Base the entire rose with Peach Sherbet. Base the center with Mississippi Mud and a touch of Royal Purple on a no. 2 round.

Highlight the top of the rose around the center with a mix of Light Mocha and a touch of Peach Sherbet on a no. 2 round. Pull the back comma stroke first, this should have more Light Mocha in the mix; then pull the comma stroke on the front of the rose.

Shade the left side and bottom of the rose with a float of Antique Rose using a no. 14 flat. Add a comma stroke to the left side with the mix mentioned above.

Float a deeper shade over the Antique Rose with thinned Royal Purple. Add two to three more highlight strokes of Light Mocha + Peach Sherbet 1:1 on the right side using a no. 2 round. Shade next to the right side with thinned Mississippi Mud on a no. 0 liner.

21 LEAVES & VINES

Base the vines and leaves with a no. 0 liner and Light Avocado.

The first highlight strokes on the leaves are pulled with thinned Hauser Medium Green on a no. 0 liner. Overstroke the comma strokes here and there with the Hauser Medium Green.

Add "stitching" lines with the brown permanent ink pen down the middle and along the right side of the leaves and next to the vine.

Add shadow strokes next to the leaves and vines with thinned Mississippi Mud on a no. 2 round.

Framed Sampler

RISE & SHINE BOX

Roosters and hens are a favorite theme for painters of American country scenes. The style of this project is loose and painterly. And the crackled basecoat helps to keep the brush-strokes casual.

Don't be afraid to give this style of painting a try—it's very liberating, and much more interesting to look at than a tight "coloring book" style. Try using a blending medium or extender, which will give you a more relaxed look in your painting because your paint will stay wet longer and your edges will be softer.

Patterns

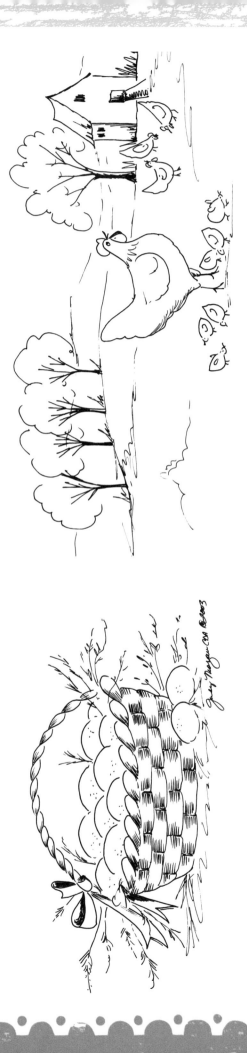

These patterns may be hand-traced
or photocopied for personal use
only. Enlarge at 222% to bring
them up to full size.

Colors & Materials

Paint: Delta Ceramcoat Acrylics

 Antique Gold

 Black

 Blue Haze

 Burnt Sienna

 Candy Bar Brown

 Gamal Green

 Light Foliage Green

 Mudstone

 Opaque Red

 Purple

 Raw Linen

 Tangerine

 Terra Cotta

 Walnut

 White

Surface

- Oval bentwood box, available from Stan Brown's and Viking Woodcrafts catalogs

Brushes

- ½-inch (13mm) oval wash brush
- no. 2 round
- nos. 6 and 8 filberts
- no. 12 Bringle Blender
- no. 0/0 liner
- no. 14 flat

Additional Supplies

- Delta Blending Medium
- Delta Ceramcoat All-purpose Sealer
- Delta Crackle Medium
- Delta Glaze Medium
- Sandpaper and tack cloth
- Dark graphite paper and stylus

Preparing the Surface

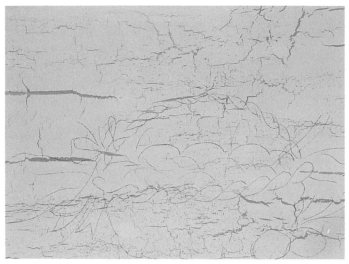

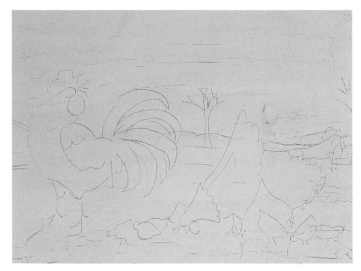

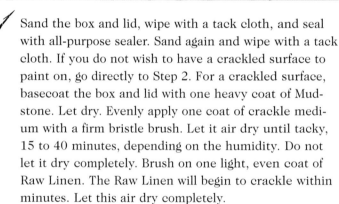

1 Sand the box and lid, wipe with a tack cloth, and seal with all-purpose sealer. Sand again and wipe with a tack cloth. If you do not wish to have a crackled surface to paint on, go directly to Step 2. For a crackled surface, basecoat the box and lid with one heavy coat of Mudstone. Let dry. Evenly apply one coat of crackle medium with a firm bristle brush. Let it air dry until tacky, 15 to 40 minutes, depending on the humidity. Do not let it dry completely. Brush on one light, even coat of Raw Linen. The Raw Linen will begin to crackle within minutes. Let this air dry completely.

2 Transfer your pattern lines with dark graphite paper.

3 Using a ½-inch (13mm) oval wash brush, apply a coat of blending medium over the back hills. Work a small area at a time. Pick up Light Foliage Green + Raw Linen 1:1 on the brush and loosely base in the back hills. Most of the color is at the top of the hills; as you move down more background should show through. Pinch out the brush with a paper towel and pick up a small amount of Blue Haze and stroke at the very top of the hills for a highlight. Brush blending medium over the foreground, then pick up Gamal Green and brush this loosely over the middle foreground area.

4 Apply blending medium over the lower foreground areas under the chickens. Pick up Antique Gold on the brush and loosely apply in these areas.

Background & Basecoating

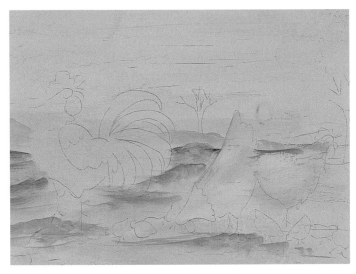

5 Pinch out the brush on a paper towel and pick up a bit of Gamal Green. Slip-slap this under the chickens' feet. This shadow "grounds" the chickens so they don't appear to be floating in midair.

6 Clean out the oval wash brush with water. Pinch out as much water as you can onto a paper towel. Apply blending medium over the sky area in the far background. Pick up a mix of Purple + White and slip-slap this color in the sky area. Pinch out the brush on a paper towel and pick up Tangerine; apply at the bottom of the sky behind the rooster. Pinch out the brush again and pick up a bit of White. Add casual strokes of White for clouds between the Purple and Tangerine.

7 The tree trunks and branches are based with Walnut + Black 1:1 on a no. 0/0 liner. Apply a shadow of Black on the left side of each trunk and a highlight of Terra Cotta to the right side of each trunk with the no. 0/0 liner.

Use a no. 12 Bringle Blender brush and Gamal Green to stipple on the tree foliage. Highlight the foliage with a stipple of Light Foliage Green at the top of the trees. Stipple a second highlight at the very top of the trees with a 1:1 mix of Light Foliage Green + Antique Gold.

8 Load a no. 8 filbert brush with Terra Cotta and base in the bodies of all the hens and the rooster. Using a no. 2 round, base in their combs and wattles with Candy Bar Brown. Base in their beaks and feet with Walnut on a no. 0/0 liner.

Rooster & Hen

9 The rooster's dark tail feathers are based with a mix of Purple + Black 1:1 on a no. 2 round. Base in the green tail feathers with Gamal Green. Base in the saddle feathers with Black.

10 Sideload a no. 8 filbert with Burnt Sienna. Shade under the wings, necks, lower bodies, and at the rear of the rooster. Your sideload strokes will be much nicer if you add a touch of blending medium to the brush.

11 Next, highlight the tops of the heads, the ends of the hen's tail feathers, and the tips of the wings with a no. 6 filbert loaded with a mix of Terra Cotta + Antique Gold 1:1. Add a tiny bit of White to the mix for an extra highlight at the very tips of the tail feathers and tips of the wings.

12 Apply the first highlight on the comb and wattle with a no. 2 round tipped into Opaque Red. Pinch out the brush on a paper towel and pick up a tiny bit of Tangerine; add this second highlight to the center of the first highlight.

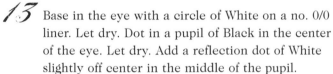

13 Base in the eye with a circle of White on a no. 0/0 liner. Let dry. Dot in a pupil of Black in the center of the eye. Let dry. Add a reflection dot of White slightly off center in the middle of the pupil.

14 To detail the purple tail feathers, mix together Purple + a touch of White, and use a no. 0/0 liner to pull a thin line of this color down the middle of each purple tail feather. On each side of this thin line, pull straight strokes of the same color at a 45-degree angle from the middle out. The feather strokes get smaller as you move towards the tip of the feather.

The green tail feathers are detailed in the same manner; mix together Gamal Green + Blue Haze 1:1 and use a no. 0/0 liner.

15 On your palette, thin Blue Haze with enough water to make it almost transparent. Pull squiggly lines on the saddle feathers using a no. 0/0 liner.

Chicks, Weeds & Egg Basket

16 With a no. 0/0 liner, base the chicks with Antique Gold. Base their feet, beaks and eyes with Walnut. Shade each chick with a no. 6 filbert sideloaded with Burnt Sienna. Pull the shade under each wing, head and under each breast. Sideload a no. 6 filbert with a mix of Antique Gold + White 2:1 and highlight the wings and the backs of the chicks.

17 Using a no. 0/0 liner with a mix of Gamal Green + Walnut 1:1, pull uneven strokes from the ground up to create the weeds. Dot the tip ends of the weeds with White.

18 On the lid of the bentwood box, base the basket with a no. 6 filbert and a mix of Antique Gold + White 1:1. Base the eggs with a no. 2 round and a mix of Raw Linen + White 1:1. Base the ribbon and bow with Purple. Shade with a mix of Purple + a touch of Black.

19 Using a no. 0/0 liner and Terra Cotta thinned with water, go over the basket weave transfer lines. Also outline the basket handle with the thinned Terra Cotta.

Basket Weave

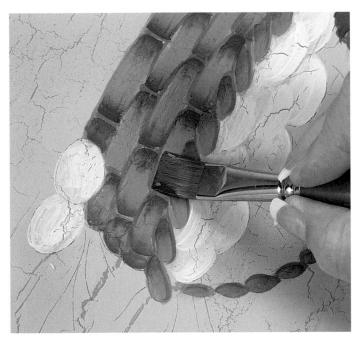

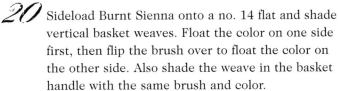

20 Sideload Burnt Sienna onto a no. 14 flat and shade vertical basket weaves. Float the color on one side first, then flip the brush over to float the color on the other side. Also shade the weave in the basket handle with the same brush and color.

21 Sideload a no. 14 flat with a mix of Antique Gold + White 2:1. Highlight the middle of each weave where it bends outward with a flip-float (see page 14). Highlight the top rim of the basket and the basket handle with the same brush and color.

22 With the same highlight mix of Antique Gold + White, load a no. 0/0 liner and pull small horizontal dry-brush strokes across the floated highlight. Do the same on the basket handle and along the top rim of the basket. Add a bit more White to the mix for a smaller and lighter second highlight.

Eggs, Ribbon & Wheat

23 Sideload a no. 14 flat with a thinned mix of Purple + a touch of Walnut. Shade between the eggs, keeping most of the shade towards the left side. Using the same brush and color, shade under the basket with the chisel edge of the brush, keeping it loose and transparent. Shade with the same brush and color next to the handle and bow.

24 Tint the left sides of the eggs with thinned Blue Haze on a no. 8 filbert. Tint the right sides with thinned Antique Gold. Use a no. 0/0 liner and thinned Burnt Sienna to dot some "freckles" here and there on the eggs.

25 Load a no. 6 filbert with a mix of Purple + White 1:1, and dry-brush highlights on the ends of the ribbons. Sideload a no. 14 flat with thinned Blue Haze and float a shine at the bends of the bow.

26 The stems of the wheat are based first with thinned Purple + Walnut 1:1 on a no. 0/0 liner. Pull straight lines behind the bow, eggs and basket. Highlight the stems with Burnt Sienna, then Antique Gold, using a no. 0/0 liner. Load the liner with Antique Gold and pull short straight strokes for the wheat grains.

Finished Box

WINTER CABINET

Here is another simple farm landscape for you that is so much fun to paint. This reminds me of New England in late fall/early winter, with its old-fashioned houses and winding country road. I added a few more easy techniques for you to try with this project, such as dotting in snow and fall leaves using a brush.

Check out the flea markets and architectural salvage yards for small furniture pieces like this wall cabinet; even an old medicine cabinet or old door would be fun to paint on. Keep your eyes open to all the possibilities.

Pattern

This pattern may be hand-traced or photocopied for personal use only.
Enlarge at 133% to bring it up to full size.

Colors & Materials

Paint: Delta Ceramcoat Acrylics

Barn Red

Black

Boston Fern

Burnt Sienna

Dark Flesh

Dusty Plum

Fleshtone

Golden Brown

Light Timberline Green

Medium Flesh

Mello Yellow

Napa Wine

Tangerine

Terra Cotta

Wedgwood Blue

White

Williamsburg Blue

White +
a touch of Black

Surface

- Small wooden wall cabinet from Pesky Bear

Brushes

- no. 14 flat
- 1½-inch (38mm) varnish brush
- no. 2 round
- no. 0/0 liner
- no. 0 liner

Sky & Hills

1 Base the sky with Wedgwood Blue. Base the back hills with Dusty Plum, the foreground with Light Timberline Green, and the road with Golden Brown. Transfer the pattern lines for the snow, trees and buildings with dark graphite paper and a stylus.

2 Sideload a no. 14 flat brush with Napa Wine and float a shade under the snow on the back hills and along the bottom of the same hills where they meet the foreground.

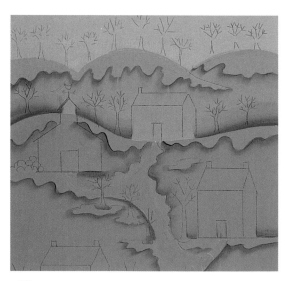

3 Sideload a no. 14 flat into Boston Fern and shade under and around the snow areas on the green foreground.

4 Dampen the sky area with water and a 1½-inch (38mm) varnish brush. Sideload the same brush with Williamsburg Blue and pull this color across the very top of the sky to deepen the blue.

Snow, Trees & Houses

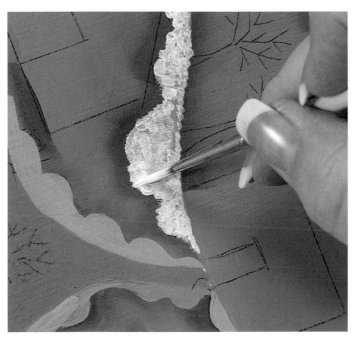

5   Base in all the snow areas with a medium value gray (White + Black 2:1) using a no. 2 round brush. Turn your surface to make it easier to stroke. Pick up more White in the brush and pounce this lighter value next to the shaded area. Gradually work the lighter snow up the drifts, letting some of the medium value gray show through.

6   Load a no. 0/0 liner with Black and base in the trees. Start at the bottom of the tree and pull towards the branches. This will keep the branches thin and delicate looking.

7   Load a no. 0/0 liner with Golden Brown and pull a highlight line down the right side of each trunk. The foliage is dotted on with a no. 0/0 liner and the following colors: Barn Red, Terra Cotta and Tangerine. Each tree is a different color. The dots are varying sizes.

8   Load a no. 2 round with Barn Red and base in the barn. Base in the yellow house with Mello Yellow. The barn will need approximately two coats to cover, the yellow house up to four coats.

House & Barn Details

9 Load a no. 2 round with Black and base in the roof, eave lines, windows and doors. Sideload a no. 14 flat with thinned Terra Cotta and shade the right side of the front of the yellow house to separate the front from the side, and float a shade under the roof eaves.

10 Load a no. 0/0 liner with Black and base in the weather vane and rooflines on the barn. Load the liner with thinned Terra Cotta and add the pediment over the door and the side columns to the yellow house.

11 Sideload a no. 14 flat with a medium value gray mix of White + a touch of Black. Float a first highlight down the center of the yellow house's roof, then flip the brush over and pull the same color next to and slightly over the previous floated highlight. Add a second highlight of White down the center of the first highlight with a no. 0/0 liner. Using a no. 14 flat and the medium value gray, pull a highlight down the left side of the door of the yellow house.

For the windowpanes, load a no. 0/0 liner with the medium value gray and pull vertical and horizontal lines through the windows. Use the same brush and color to stroke highlight lines on top of the barn roofs.

Load a no. 0/0 liner with White and outline the barn windows and doors, and the left sides of the yellow house's windows. Draw X's in the barn's windows and doors, and add a highlight to the weather vane.

Pumpkins & Chimneys

12 Use a no. 0/0 liner and Tangerine to pull vertical siding lines down the barn. You may need to thin the Tangerine with water so it flows off the liner brush.

The pumpkins at the side of the barn are dotted on with the end of a brush handle dipped in Terra Cotta. The size of the end of the brush handle determines the size of the dot. Let the dots dry. Use a no. 0/0 liner tipped in Tangerine to stroke a small highlight dot on the right side of each pumpkin dot. Let dry. The second highlight is a smaller dot of Mello Yellow. Add stems to the top of each pumpkin with Golden Brown. Pick up White on a no. 0/0 liner and dot in snow on the top of the pumpkin pile.

13 Use a no. 0/0 liner and Barn Red to base in the chimney on the yellow house. Load a liner with the medium value gray you used for the roof highlight, and pull a squiggly line of smoke from the chimney up. The line breaks into dots as it gets above the trees. Highlight the smoke line with the same brush and White.

For the twiggy bushes along the foundation, load a liner with Boston Fern and pull short branching strokes. Dot White across the bushes for snow.

Shadows, Fence, Road & Brick House

14 Load a no. 0/0 liner with a mix of Napa Wine + a touch of Black and paint the shadows of the trees across the snow. Keep this color thin and transparent. The shadow begins at the base of the tree and mimics the shape of the trunks and branches.

Use the same brush and White thinned with water to line in the fence. Pull the vertical fence posts first, then pull the rails. Note that the fence posts must be parallel with the sides of the painting, no matter how many hills and dales the fence follows. Base in the road and paths with Terra Cotta.

15 Sideload a no. 14 flat with Burnt Sienna and float a shadow along the edge of the road and paths. Keep the shadow at the top of the U-shaped section and along the left side of the rest of the road. Also shade under the doors of the house and barn.

Use a no. 2 round and thinned White to dot in snow down the middle of the road.

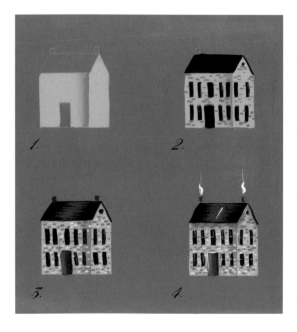

BRICK HOUSE

1. Base the walls with Fleshtone on a no. 2 round brush. Sideload a no. 14 flat with Dark Flesh and float a shadow on the right front corner of the house.

2. Start the brick pattern with a no. 0 liner loaded in Dark Flesh. Apply the bricks in a random, open pattern, leaving room for more bricks of lighter colors. Base in the roof, windows and door with Black.

3. Highlight the center of the roof with a flip-float of a dark value gray (Black + White 2:1). Use the same brush and color to float a highlight down the left side of the door. Base the chimneys with Barn Red on the left side and Terra Cotta on the right side using a no. 0 liner. Add some lighter color bricks with a no. 0 liner and Medium Flesh.

4. Mix a light value gray (White + a touch of Black). Pull a line of smoke out of each chimney. Add more White to the brush and over-stroke the smoke. Pull a straight highlight line through the middle of the roof highlight with a medium value gray (White + Black 2:1). With the same mix on a no. 0 liner, outline the windows and door, and add vertical and horizontal windowpanes.

Finished Cabinet

APPLE VALLEY CLOCK

There is something so charming about a simple folk art landscape. One of my favorite artists who painted so well in this style was Warren Kimble. In fact, my souvenir from a trip to New England several years ago was an original Warren Kimble landscape purchased from the man himself, after a personal tour of his studio. It was folk art nirvana.

I have adapted the clock project to a small framed piece, just to give you an idea of what you can do with a basic design. Add a little here, take away an element there and you can make this design fit a multitude of shapes and surfaces.

Pattern

This pattern may be hand-traced or photocopied for personal use only.
Enlarge at 200% to bring it up to full size.

Colors & Materials

Paint: Delta Ceramcoat Acrylics

Black

Black Green

Burnt Sienna

Calypso Orange

Dark Chocolate

Dark Victorian Teal

Eucalyptus

Forest Green

Hippo Grey

Lemon Grass

Light Ivory

Light Victorian Teal

Mustard

Old Parchment

Spice Tan

Tangerine

Terra Cotta

Timberline Green

Tompte Red

White

Surface

- 16-inch (41cm) round wooden plate with beaded edge, available from Stan Brown and Viking Woodcrafts catalogs.
- Clock works available at any craft or hobby store.

Brushes

- nos. 6 and 8 filberts
- nos. 0 and 2 rounds
- nos. 14 and 16 flats
- nos. 0 and 0/0 liners
- no. 8 Bringle Blender

Additional Supplies

- Brown permanent ink pen, size .01
- Light and dark graphite paper and stylus

Sky & Hills

1 Using a no. 8 filbert for the larger areas and a no. 2 round for the smaller areas, base the sky with Light Victorian Teal. Base the farthest hills with Lemon Grass, the next line of hills with Eucalyptus, the hill in the middle with Mustard, the hill on the right with Timberline Green, and the hill on the left with Forest Green. Base the foreground field with Spice Tan.

Base the border in Old Parchment. The bead along the outside rim of the clock and the back of the clock are based with Black Green on a no. 6 filbert.

2 Transfer the pattern lines with light graphite paper on the darker areas, and dark graphite on the lighter areas.

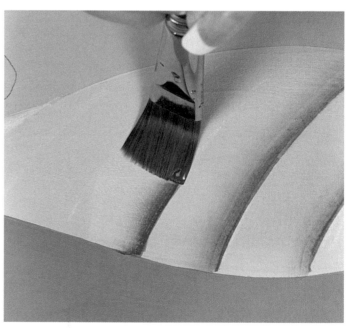

3 Sideload a no. 16 flat into Light Ivory. The clouds are large C-strokes, with the largest in the center and gradually decreasing in size towards the sides.

4 The furrows on the back hill are painted with a sideload float of Forest Green on a no. 16 flat. Pull the float from the bottom up over the hill, reloading in Forest Green for each furrow.

Apple Trees

5 Load a no. 0/0 liner with Dark Chocolate and base the tree trunks. The foliage on the trees is stippled on with the Bringle Blender brush and Forest Green. Load a no. 0 liner in Forest Green and stroke some weeds up from the furrows in the middle hill.

6 To shade the lower right sides of the trees, stipple Black Green on with the Bringle Blender. The highlights on the upper left sides are stippled on with the same brush and Lemon Grass. This gives the feeling of bright sunshine on the trees.

7 The apples are dotted on with the end of a stylus dipped in Tompte Red. You can do about 3 apples before you must dip into the paint again. On a few of the apples, add tiny reflection dots with Light Ivory. Paint in the shadows under the trees with thinned Forest Green on a no. 0/0 liner.

Field & Farmhouse

8 Load a no. 0/0 liner with thinned Burnt Sienna and pull wiggly diagonal lines for furrows across the middle field.

9 Base the farmhouse with a no. 2 round and Old Parchment. Base the foundation wall and the chimneys with Hippo Grey. Base the roof, windows and door with a no. 2 round loaded in Black.

Sideload a no. 14 flat with thinned Burnt Sienna and float a shadow down the front corner of the house. When dry, float the same color under the eaves of the roof.

10 To paint the rocks on the chimneys and foundation wall, use a no. 0/0 liner to dot in the rocks in a random fashion. Start with the lighter rocks first; these are a brush-mix of Hippo Grey plus Light Ivory. Add a touch of Burnt Sienna to that mix for the mid-value rocks. The darkest rocks are Burnt Sienna plus a touch of Black. Use this same dark mix to add a shadow line along the right sides of the chimneys.

11 The darker roof highlight is a flip-float (see page 14) of Black plus a touch of Light Ivory on a no. 14 flat. Add a highlight of Light Ivory down the middle of the floated highlight. Use a no. 0/0 liner and the darker highlight mix to outline the door and windows, and to line in the windowpanes. See step 13 on page 69 for instructions on painting the smoke rising from the chimneys.

12 Base in the bushes along the foundation with Black Green on a no. 2 round. You will need two coats to cover. Highlight the tops of the bushes with Forest Green tipped into Lemon Grass on a no. 8 Bringle Blender; pounce this on the top edges of the bushes.

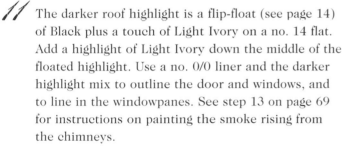

13 Load a no. 2 round with thinned Black Green and sketch in a path in a tight zigzag from the top of the hill down. As you move down the hill, the paint will become more transparent and fade away.

Barn & Pumpkin Field

14 Paint the barn following the instructions on pages 67-69 in the "Winter Cabinet" project. The colors for this barn are Tompte Red, Hippo Grey, Black and White.

15 The autumn trees are painted the same way as the trees in the Winter Cabinet project; see page 67. Base in the trunks with Dark Chocolate. Dot on the leaves with Terra Cotta, Calypso Orange and Tangerine. Start with the darkest color and end with the lightest.

16 The furrows in the pumpkin field are a flip-float (see page 14) of Burnt Sienna on a no. 14 flat brush.
   The road is shaded with a sideload of Burnt Sienna as well; float one side first in a zigzag motion pulling the color across the road. Let this dry well before floating the other side in the same way.

17 Load a no. 0/0 liner with Forest Green and pull squiggly vines over the shaded furrows. Pull some additional vines with Black Green.
   Base in the fences with a no. 0/0 liner and Light Ivory following the instructions in Step 14 of the Winter Cabinet project on page 70.

Pumpkins & Border Design

18 Load a no. 0 round with Tangerine and base in the pumpkins. Highlight the left side of each pumpkin with a mix of Calypso Orange and Tangerine by painting small C-strokes with a no. 0 round.

19 Paint the leaves in one little stroke using Forest Green for most of them, and Black Green for the rest. Highlight the leaves with dots of Eucalyptus. The sheep in the field are painted using Hippo Grey, Black and White (see steps 13 and 14 on page 46).

20 Base the clock numbers with Black using a no. 0 round. Add an offset shadow number with thinned Dark Chocolate. Base the vines with a no. 0/0 liner and Dark Chocolate.

21 Load a no. 0 round with thinned Timberline Green. Base in the leaves with two strokes; start at the base of the leaf and pull forward, then start the second stroke at the base next to the first stroke and pull side-by-side. If there is a tiny space between the two strokes, just leave it; there is no need to fill in the entire leaf.

Border Design, continued

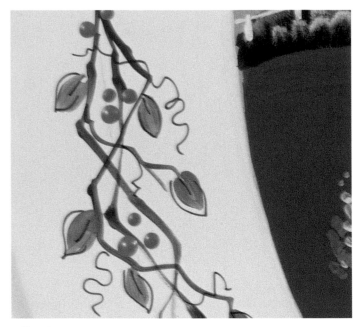

22 The berries are dotted on with the brush handle of a no. 0 round and Terra Cotta. Dab on about three berries at a time. Each berry will get slightly smaller as you go. I like to do about three together in a cluster, and then a single berry here and there.

23 Use a brown permanent ink pen to ink around the leaves and vines. Add a few curly tendrils here and there.

24 Load a no. 0 round brush with Black and paint the "lifeline" around the entire clock that divides the border from the middle.

Here is a portion of the "Apple Valley" design on a different surface. This is just a square framed piece, and I glued some twigs on the frame for a more rustic look. Don't be afraid to adapt designs to fit almost any shape and surface you want.

TREE OF LIFE DOOR CROWN

This piece was patterned a fter Pennsylvania Dutch "frakturs"—handwritten documents from the last half of the 18th century that recorded births and baptisms. The scribe often added decorative embellishments, such as the tree of life and folk art birds. I tweaked the palette a bit for a more modern look, so the colors are brighter and have more impact than the sedate earth tones of the original frakturs from 200 years ago. The design has a lot of repetition—easy for the beginner painter.

Pattern

This pattern may be hand-traced or photocopied for personal use only. Enlarge at 185% to bring it up to full size.

Purple Bird

Red Bird

Daisy

Blue Bird

Heart Tulip

5

4

3

Judy Morgan CDA ©2003

1   2   6

Colors & Materials

Paint: Delta Ceramcoat Acrylics

Apple Green

Bittersweet Orange

Black

Black Green

Cardinal Red

Cloudberry Tan

Colonial Blue

Grape

Jade Green

Manganese Blue

Mello Yellow

Periwinkle Blue

Poppy Orange

Rhythm 'N Blue

Spice Brown

Vibrant Green

White

Surface

- Wooden door crown, available from Unique Woods

Brushes

- no. 8 flat
- no. 14 flat
- no. 0 round
- no. 2 round
- no. 6 filbert
- no. 0/0 liner
- 1-inch (25mm) basing brush

Additional Supplies

- Stylus
- Dark graphite paper
- ½-inch (13mm) check stencil

Basecoating

Basecoat the entire door crown with Cloudberry Tan, using the 1-inch (25mm) basing brush. Let dry and then transfer the pattern. Note the pattern labels on page 86, which are used to identify the design elements referred to in these instructions.

Base the flowerpot in Mello Yellow, using a no. 14 flat. Then base the vines and the large leaves in Black Green. For the vines use a no. 0/0 liner; for the leaves a no. 2 round. The birds are all based with a no. 2 round. Base the blue birds' bodies with Rhythm 'N Blue and their wings with Colonial Blue. Base the purple birds' bodies with Grape and their wings with Colonial Blue. Base the red birds' bodies Cardinal Red and their wings with Jade Green. Base the center of the top heart-shaped tulip with a no. 2 round and Jade Green. Base the line around the heart shape with a no. 0 round and Poppy Orange. Base the scalloped border outside the heart shape with a no. 0

round and Vibrant Green. Use a no. 0 round for all the basing listed below:

TULIP 1: Base the center with Cardinal Red and the outside with Rhythm 'N Blue.

TULIP 2: Base the center petal with Rhythm 'N Blue and the outside petals with Vibrant Green.

TULIP 3: Base the center petal with Jade Green and the outside petals with Black Green.

TULIP 4: Base the center with Jade Green and the outside with Vibrant Green.

TULIP 5: Base the center petal with Rhythm 'N Blue and the outside petals with Cardinal Red.

TULIP 6: Base the same as Tulip 3.

DAISIES: Base the donut shape with Bittersweet Orange and the center with Spice Brown.

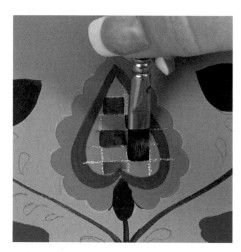

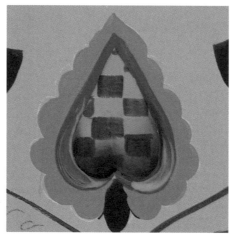

1 Place the check stencil over the center of the heart-shaped tulip and outline the pattern on the center with light pencil lines. Load a no. 8 flat brush with thinned Manganese Blue and paint alternate rectangles to form a check pattern. For the smaller areas, fill in with Manganese Blue and a no. 0 round brush.

2 Shade the bottom of the heart shape with a float of Manganese Blue on a no. 14 flat brush. Highlight the curves of the Poppy Orange outline area with a stroke of Bittersweet Orange on each side, using a no. 0 round.

3 Sideload a no. 14 flat brush with thinned Black Green. Shade under the Poppy Orange outline, on the Vibrant Green. Highlight the green area with a no. 0 round brush loaded with Apple Green. Pull C-strokes around the heart on each scallop. Pull a straight comma stroke of Apple Green on the calyx. Then pull three straight comma strokes at the top of the heart-shaped tulip, painting the center stroke first and then the outside strokes.

4 Sideload Manganese Blue onto a no. 14 flat brush and float a shade under the wings of the blue bird. Load a no. 2 round brush with Colonial Blue and pull straight comma strokes on the tail. Use a no. 0 round brush and Colonial Blue to place short comma strokes of graduated size on the bird's breast and one comma stroke under the bird's chin.

5 Place the check stencil over the wing. You have the option of tracing the checks on with pencil and basing with a brush or using a small stencil brush to apply the paint. Be careful not to get paint onto the background. Base in the checks with thinned Manganese Blue. Base in the eye with a no. 0 round brush and White. This is a teardrop shape with the widest part away from the beak. Base the beak and feet with a no. 0/0 round brush and Spice Brown.

6 Add White to Colonial Blue and highlight the breast and tail comma strokes with a no. 0 round. Place a Black dot in the eye for a pupil. Add shade strokes of thinned Black on the beak and feet. Outline the eye with a Black C-stroke.

7 TULIP 1

Load a no. 0 round with Poppy Orange and pull large strokes from the base of the centers toward the tips. Let dry. Then pick up Bittersweet Orange on the same brush and overstroke the first comma strokes with a smaller comma strokes.

8 TULIP 1

Load a no. 0 round with Periwinkle Blue and pull strokes from the base of the outside petals toward the tips. These strokes are on the petals closest to the heart-shaped tulip.

Tulips 2, 3 & 4

9 TULIP 2

Sideload a no. 14 flat brush with thinned Manganese Blue and float a shade on the bottom edge of the center. Sideload the no. 14 flat brush into Black Green and shade the bottom edge of each green petal.

10 TULIP 3

Sideload a no. 14 flat brush into thinned Black Green and shade the bottom of the tulip center. Load a no. 2 round brush into Colonial Blue and place two comma strokes over the center area. The first stroke is toward the outside edge. The second, smaller stroke is at the center. Add three straight comma strokes just above the tip.

11 TULIP 3

Load a no. 2 round brush into Vibrant Green and pull a comma stroke on each Black Green petal toward the inside edge. Let dry. Then load a no. 0 round brush with Apple Green and pull a smaller comma stroke over the first.

12 TULIP 4

Sideload a no. 14 flat brush with thinned Black Green. Float a shade of the Black Green on the top side of the center over the Jade Green basecoat. Float the same color over the base of the outside petals.

13 TULIP 4

Load a no. 0 round in Colonial Blue and pull two comma strokes over the light side of the center. Load into Apple Green and pull two comma strokes from the outside petal tips toward the base. Add three straight comma strokes of Colonial Blue at the tip.

Tulip 5, Daisies & Leaves

14 TULIP 5

Sideload a no. 14 flat brush with Manganese Blue and float a shade next to the red outside petals. Load a no. 0 round brush with Colonial Blue and pull two straight comma strokes in the tulip tip. Load the same brush with Rhythm 'N Blue and pull three small straight comma strokes above the tulip tip.

15 TULIP 5
Load a no. 0 round into Poppy Orange and pull strokes from the bases of the outside red petals toward the tips. While the paint is wet, pick up Bitter-sweet Orange and overstroke with a smaller stroke. In the same way, highlight the center petal, but start the strokes at the tip and pull to the base.

16 DAISIES
Load a no. 0 round brush into Mello Yellow and pull straight strokes over the top half of the donut-shaped daisy. Pinch out the brush and pick up Bitter-sweet Orange + Mello Yellow, blending on the palette. Then pull the remaining petals on the bottom half.

17 DAISY CENTER
Load the large end of a stylus with Poppy Orange and apply pollen dots on the top half of the daisy center. Clean off the stylus and pick up Mello Yellow. Apply dots to the bottom half of the center.

18 LEAVES
Load a no. 2 round into Vibrant Green. Pull a long stroke from the tip of each large leaf toward the base.

19 Switch to a no. 0 round and pick up Vibrant Green. Pull straight comma strokes from the outside leaf edges, angled toward the centers. Pinch out the brush, pick up Apple Green and pull smaller overstrokes.

Filler Strokes & Flowerpot

20 FILLER STROKES
Use a no. 0 round loaded in Vibrant Green to apply the filler comma strokes. Pinch out the brush and overstroke a few filler strokes with Apple Green.

21 FLOWERPOT
Apply the check pattern with dark graphite paper, keeping the lines light for easier removal later. A ruler helps keep the lines straight. Load a no. 2 round into thinned Cloudberry Tan and base alternating checks, keeping the color transparent. Let the checks dry.

22 Sideload a no. 14 flat into Cloudberry Tan and float a shade on the inside edge of the flowerpot, each side of the pot and along the bottom edge.

23 Sideload the same no. 14 flat with more Cloudberry Tan and shade the bottom edge of each check. Load a no. 0 round into Cloudberry Tan and pull short, uneven lines over the floated shade.

Detailing

24 To make the design pop, load a no. 0 round into thinned Spice Brown. Outline around some design details, such as the top sides of the daisies, the shade sides of the leaves and tulips, and under the birds.

25 Use a no. 6 filbert loaded with Black Green and base the coved edge of the door crown.

Erase any leftover pattern lines before applying a protective finish with water-based varnish.

Finished Door Crown

SNOWMEN BOX

Nothing says winter like a gathering of jolly snowmen warming their mittens over a toasty fire. You can display snowman-decorated items like this mitten box from November through the entire winter season, including the holidays. You have to put Santa away after Christmas, but these comical snowmen can hang around and keep you smiling for months. Why not keep your own mittens in this adorable box?

Patterns

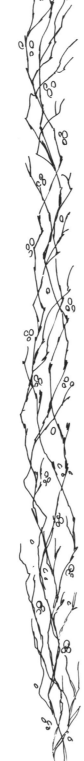

These patterns may be hand-traced or photo-copied for personal use only. Enlarge at 185% to bring them up to full size.

Colors & Materials

Paint: Delta Ceramcoat Acrylics

Adriatic Blue

Bittersweet Orange

Black

Blue Haze

Blue Mist

Blue Wisp

Bonnie Blue

Brown Velvet

Deep River Green

Fruit Punch

Jade Green

Lavender

Light Ivory

Mallard Green

Straw

Tangerine

Surface

- Rectangular lidded wooden box, available from Sechtem's Wood Products

Brushes

- no. 4 duster/stippler
- no. 14 flat
- no. 0 round
- no. 2 round
- no. 8 Bringle Blender
- 1-inch (25mm) basing brush

Additional Supplies

- Blue painters tape
- Light graphite paper
- Stylus
- Water-based varnish

Border & Snow Drifts

1 Base the entire box with Bonnie Blue, using a 1-inch (25mm) basing brush. Let dry. Measure off the inset on the lid, about 1¼ inch (32mm) from the edge, and tape off with blue painters tape. Base the outside border with Deep River Green. Let dry, but do not remove the tape.

2 Wet the border area one section at a time. Wet a no. 4 duster/stippler brush with water and squeeze out the excess with a paper towel. Pick up Blue Haze, dab off the excess paint onto a paper towel, then stipple onto the border. Let dry, and remove the painters tape.

3 Transfer the individual snowdrifts and the snowmen outlines with light graphite paper and a stylus. Using a no. 8 Bringle Blender brush, pick up Blue Wisp and stipple in the snowdrifts. Start at the top of each drift and work down. Leave some background showing through, as this will be part of the shaded area.

4 Still using the no. 8 Bringle Blender brush, pick up the highlight color of Blue Mist. The highlight is kept toward the top of each drift and gradually blended into the first stippling of Blue Wisp.

Snowmen, Trees & House

5 Stipple in the snowmen with the Bringle Blender brush and Blue Wisp. This first stippling is an even coat with some background showing through. Pinch out the Bringle Blender brush and pick up Blue Mist. This highlight color is kept toward the middle of each snowman and blended toward the outside edges. This effect makes the snowmen appear round. Do the same highlight stipple effect on the snowmen's heads.

6 The final highlight is done with the Bringle Blender and Light Ivory. Add a touch of this color on the top of each drift and at the center of the first highlight on each snowman.

7 Using a no. 14 flat brush and thinned Adriatic Blue, float a shadow along the path edges. Float a shadow to separate the snowmen from the background.

8 Using a no. 0 round loaded with Brown Velvet, base in the tree trunks, the tree limbs and the house. Use the no. 0 round loaded with Black to base in the roof, chimney, windows and door.

House & Snowman Details

9 Using a no. 0 round and Brown Velvet + a touch of Straw, pull a highlight line on the left side of each tree trunk. With the same brush and color mix, pull vertical lines down the front of the house to mimic siding. Load a no. 0 round with Straw and place tiny rectangles for windowpanes to mimic interior light coming through each window. Also place one tiny rectangle of Straw on the top center of the door. Load a no. 0 round with Blue Mist and pull a slightly horizontal line of chimney smoke. Use the same brush and color to dot snow on the rooftop. Pull vertical lines of the same color at the lower roof eaves for icicles. Dot snow into the tree branches as well.

10 Load a no. 0 round into Brown Velvet and base in the snowmen's twig arms. Load a no. 0 round into Jade Green and base in the earmuffs and mittens of the snowman on the right. Base the scarf with the same brush, using Mallard Green. Use a no. 0 round and Black to line in the earmuff band.

11 Highlight the top half of the earmuffs with brush dots of Jade Green applied with a no. 0 round. Then pull a highlight stroke of Jade Green across the top of each mitten. Shade the underside of the earmuffs with a float of thinned Mallard Green, using a no. 14 flat. Shade the underside of each mitten with a stroke of Mallard Green, using a no. 0 round. With the same brush and color, pull short straight strokes of fringe at the ends of the scarf.

Snowman Details & Fire

12 The plaid is applied with a no. 0 round and Lavender. Pull all the vertical lines first, then finish with the horizontal lines. Add a few Lavender straight strokes over the fringe.

13 Highlight the top of the earmuff band with a line of Light Ivory. Base the carrot nose with Bittersweet Orange, using a no. 0 round. Let dry, then highlight the top edge with Straw. Base the eyes, mouth and buttons with Black. Highlight with tiny shine dots of Light Ivory, using the tip of a no. 0 round.

14 Base the logs with Brown Velvet using a no. 2 round. Base the fire with the same brush and Straw.

15 Shade the logs to separate them with Brown Velvet + a touch of Black on a no. 14 flat. Highlight with strokes of Brown Velvet + Straw on a no. 2 round. Highlight the flames with Straw + Light Ivory on a no. 2 round, pulling the strokes from the fire's base.

Bushes, Lifeline & Top Hat

16 Base the bushes with a no. 0 round brush and Brown Velvet. Start at the bottom of the bush and pull up. Finish with stylus dots of Bittersweet Orange at the ends of the branches.

17 Separate the inset from the border with a lifeline of Black on a no. 0 round brush.

18 TOP HAT

A. Using a no. 0 round brush, base the hat with Black and the hatband with Fruit Punch.

B. Highlight down the center of the hat crown with a flip-float of Blue Wisp. Continue the highlight over the hat brim with the same flip-float of Blue Wisp. Highlight the center of the hatband with a flip-float of Fruit Punch + Straw, using a no. 14 flat brush.

C. Add an extra thin highlight line of Blue Wisp + Light Ivory to the center of the hat crown and brim using a no. 0 liner. With the same brush, add an extra highlight of Straw to the center of the hatband.

Berry & Twig Border

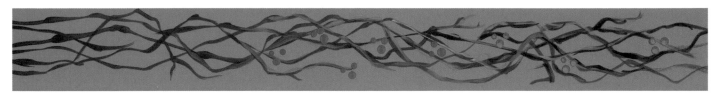

19 For the berry and twig border, begin the twigs using a no. 0 round and Brown Velvet. To get an uneven, knotty look, apply and release pressure on the brush as you pull the strokes. Highlight the twigs with overstrokes of Brown Velvet + Straw, using the same brush.

　　The berries are brush-handle dots of Bittersweet Orange. Dot on about three at a time with one dip into the paint. The berries will get progressively smaller as you go along. If you want all your berries to be the same size, dip into the paint for each one.

20 Let all the paint dry. Then tape off the twig border with blue painters tape. Apply fly-specking (see page 13) over the snowmen scene with Blue Mist to simulate falling snow. Let dry. Erase any leftover pattern lines. Protect the finished box with water-based varnish.

Finished Mitten Box

FRENCH FLORAL BUCKET

I simply love the look of antique French enamelware, and especially this shade of green. Metal buckets like these are used by florists to stand flowerstems in water while on display.

I purchased this bucket from the gardening department at my local Ikea store. They have lots of inexpensive galvanized metal pieces to choose from. If you do not have an Ikea close by, try your local home improvement store or gardening center. Or paint the rose design on a tray, round box or plate.

Patterns

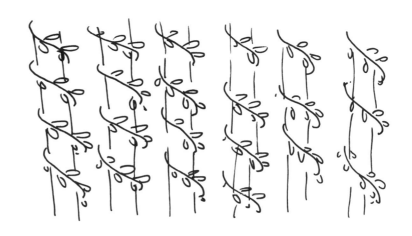

These patterns may be hand-traced or photocopied for personal use only. Enlarge at 120% to bring them up to full size.

Colors & Materials

Paint: Delta Ceramcoat Acrylics

Apple Green

Avalon Blue

Fruit Punch

Gamal Green

Light Foliage Green

Light Ivory

Medium Foliage Green

Pineapple Yellow

Poppy Orange

Raw Sienna

Rouge

Sweetheart Blush

Turquoise

Turquoise + Light Ivory (1:1)

Avalon Blue + a touch of Turquoise

Avalon Blue + Gamal Green (1:1)

Fruit Punch + Sweetheart Blush (1:1)

Surface

- Galvanized metal flower bucket, available from Ikea or your local home and garden center.

Brushes

- no. 4 duster/stippler
- no. 2 round
- no. 6 round
- no. 0 liner
- no. 8 filbert
- ¾-inch (19mm) flat
- 1-inch (25mm) wash

Additional Supplies

- Gray sandable metal primer
- Delta Faux Finish Glaze
- White chalk pencil or soapstone pencil
- Light graphite paper
- Stylus
- Water-based varnish

Preparation & Basecoating

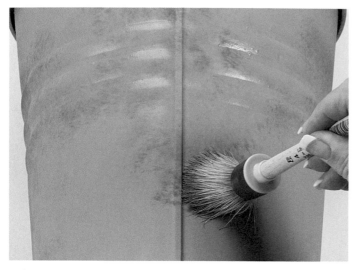

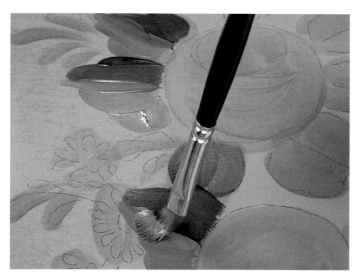

1 Wash the metal bucket in warm soapy water and let it dry thoroughly. Spray with gray sandable metal primer. Basecoat with Light Foliage Green.

Wet the no. 4 duster/stippler brush thoroughly in water. Pinch out the excess and dress the brush in Delta Faux Finish Glaze. Now pick up a small amount of Raw Sienna and dab over the top and bottom of the bucket sides, about four inches (10.2cm) on each end. This gives it a slightly rusty, aged look.

2 Transfer the pattern lines with light graphite paper. Undercoat the entire design with thinned Raw Sienna, making sure you can still see the pattern lines.

3 Load a no. 8 filbert brush with Gamal Green and base in the large leaves. While the leaves are still wet, pick up Light Foliage Green in the same brush and blend it onto the left side of the leaves. Pull the color from the outside in.

4 Base and blend all the large leaves around the center roses.

Leaves & Roses

5 Load a no. 6 round brush with Medium Foliage Green and then tip into Apple Green. Pull highlight strokes over the light sides of the large leaves, letting the base color show through. Pull these strokes from the outside in, toward the vein.

6 Pinch out the brush and tip into Pineapple Yellow. Dry-brush this second highlight on the outside edges of the leaves. Load a no. 0 liner brush Apple Green and paint a center vein line and smaller lines of the same color, pulling at an angle toward the center.

7 Dress a no. 2 round brush in the Faux Finish Glaze. Pick up a small amount of Avalon Blue and apply one or two strokes to the shade side of each leaf. Let the background color dominate.

8 Base the roses with a no. 8 filbert loaded in Rouge. While the roses are still wet, pick up Sweetheart Blush and blend it into the shade side. Pick up Poppy Orange in the same brush and stroke it into the center. Don't worry if the rose looks a little messy at this time—mine did too.

Roses, continued

9 If the shade side of your rose is not dark enough, take this opportunity to deepen it by sideloading into Sweetheart Blush with a ¾-inch flat brush and floating more color on the darker side. Load a no. 2 round into Fruit Punch and tip into Light Ivory, then pull a comma stroke on each side of the rose back. Pull an extra stroke behind the previous two strokes. Pinch out the excess color and pull some crosshatch lines under the strokes.

10 Using the same colors and brush, pull several strokes on the front side of the center.

11 Make sure the paint is dry before proceeding. Then chalk in the two main front petals. The arrows in the photo are not needed—they just show you the direction in which to paint the strokes in steps 12 and 13.

12 Load a no. 6 round into Faux Finish Glaze and Fruit Punch + Sweetheart Blush (1:1). Then tip into Light Ivory. Pull strokes from the center out, leaving a lighter color value in the center and keeping the darker value on the outside.

13 Now add a second layer of petals. This time add a bit more Light Ivory to the brush tip. Pull this layer slightly below the first. Start at the center and work out, again leaving the lightest values in the middle.

14 Sideload a ¾-inch flat brush into Sweetheart Blush and float next to the top edge of the petals and at the bottom of the rose.

15 Load a no. 2 round into Faux Finish Glaze + Fruit Punch and tip into Light Ivory. Pull a large comma stroke on each side of the rose throat.

16 Pull additional comma strokes along the outside edge of the rose. Start at the top and work down, overlapping as you go.

17 Pull more of the same comma strokes on the other side of the rose.

Roses & Blue Flowers

18 There are two remaining strokes at the bottom of the rose. Pull one on the right side of center and one on the left, slightly overlapping in the middle.

19 The center is finished with three straight comma strokes and a single brush-handle dot. Use a no. 2 round brush loaded in Poppy Orange + Pineapple Yellow (1:1). The dot goes at the bottom of the three strokes.

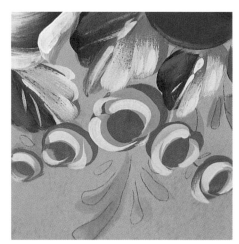

20 Base the blue flowers with a no. 2 round loaded into Avalon Blue + Gamal Green (1:1).

21 Load a no. 2 round into Avalon Blue + Turquoise (1:1). Pull two large C-strokes to create outside petals.

22 Do not wash out the brush. Pick up Turquoise + Light Ivory (1:1) and blend on the palette. Overstroke the first C-strokes without completely covering them.

23 Load a no. 0 liner into Turquoise and pull four straight comma strokes into the flower center. Finish with an oval dot of Raw Sienna on a no. 0 liner. Let dry. Tip the same brush into Pineapple Yellow and highlight the center dot.

24 Load a no. 2 round brush in Avalon Blue + Gamal Green (1:1) and base in the yellow flowers. Let dry. To highlight, place a comma stroke of Avalon Blue + a touch of Turquoise across the front of the flower using the same brush.

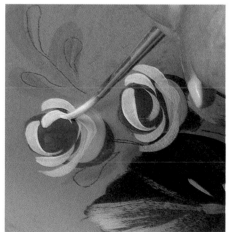

25 Add a touch of Light Ivory to the highlight mix used in step 24 and overstroke the comma stroke.

26 Load a no. 0 liner into Pineapple Yellow. Paint one large C-stroke across the flower back. Then paint one on each side. Add two smaller strokes of Pineapple Yellow in the flower throat.

27 To paint the daisies, load a no. 0 liner into Light Ivory + Faux Finish Glaze. Pull the petals from the outside in, toward the center of the flower.

Daisies, Comma Strokes & Striped Border

28 Add a brush dot of Pineapple at the centers of the little daisies.

29 Load a no. 0 liner with Medium Foliage Green + Gamal Green (1:1) and pull comma strokes in the negative spaces throughout the design. Let dry. Overstroke a few of the comma strokes with Apple Green.

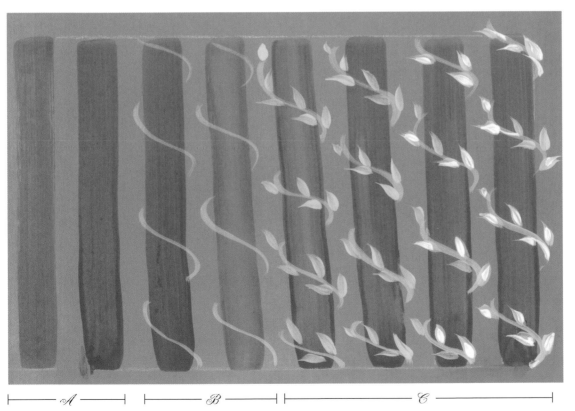

├── *A* ──┤ ├── *B* ──┤ ├───────── *C* ─────────┤

30 STRIPED BORDER

A. Load a ¾-inch (19mm) flat with Medium Foliage Green thinned with Faux Finish Glaze. Pull evenly spaced vertical stripes around the top of the bucket.

B. Load a no. 0 liner in Apple Green. Pull S-shaped twining vines around each stripe.

C. Then pull tiny leaves next to the vine. Let dry. Highlight a few of the leaves with Apple Green + Light Ivory on a no. 0 liner.

Floral Border

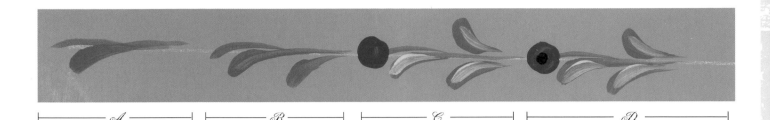

| A | B | C | D |

31 FLORAL BORDER

A. Chalk a horizontal line around the bucket under the striped border. This will help you keep your painted border straight. Pull stem lines with a no. 0 liner loaded in Medium Foliage Green.

B. Pull comma-stroke leaves with the same brush and color.

C. Overstroke the comma strokes with Apple Green and base in the flowers with Avalon Blue.

D. Add a dot of Gamal Green in the centers.

32 Erase any leftover pattern lines before applying a protective finish with water-based varnish.

Finished Flower Bucket

CORNUCOPIA

The cornucopia is a favorite subject for me. It represents abundance and life's rich blessings. That's why we see the cornucopia motif so often at Thanksgiving.

Fruit is so much fun to paint and not at all difficult. I've simplified the whole process down to three or four steps for each type, and you only have to deal with three values: the base color, a shade and a highlight. The highlight is applied with a stipple technique, which is perhaps the easiest and fastest way to highlight large objects like fruit.

Pattern

This pattern may be hand-traced or photocopied for personal use only. Enlarge at 185% to bring it up to full size.

Colors & Materials

Paint: Delta Ceramcoat Acrylics

Apple Green

Black

Candy Bar Brown

Dusty Plum

Empire Gold

Forest Green

Fruit Punch

Grape

Light Ivory

Medium Foliage Green

Red Iron Oxide

Rhythm 'N Blue

Spice Brown

Spice Tan

Terra Cotta

Vintage Wine

Surface

- Oval bentwood box, available from Stan Brown's and Viking Woodcraft catalogs.

Brushes

- no. 2 round
- no. 0 round
- no. 14 flat
- no. 12 Bringle Blender
- 1-inch (25mm) basing brush
- no. 6 filbert
- 1½-inch (38mm) flat sky wash

Additional Supplies

- Light and dark graphite paper
- ½-inch (13mm) check stencil
- Delta Blending Medium
- Water-based varnish

Basecoating, Cherries & Cornucopia

Basecoat the box and lid with Black and a 1-inch (25mm) basing brush. Be sure to keep the Black really thinned out with water. It may help to wet the surface with clean water before applying the color. When the paint is dry, transfer the basic pattern lines with light graphite paper.

CHERRIES

1. Base the cherry stem with Spice Brown, using a no. 0 round brush. Base the cherries with Red Iron Oxide and then re-base with Fruit Punch.

2. Sideload a no. 14 flat with Candy Bar Brown and float a shade on the right side of each cherry. Add a tiny Candy Bar Brown C-stroke where stem meets cherry.

3. Highlight the stem with Empire Gold and a no. 0 round. Dampen a no. 12 Bringle Blender with water and pick up a touch of Empire Gold. Tap off the excess paint on a paper towel and stipple a highlight on each cherry.

CORNUCOPIA

1. Base the cornucopia with Spice Tan and a no. 14 flat. Use a no. 2 round on the twisted end. Let dry. Then transfer the ribbed part of the basket weave with dark graphite paper. Use Spice Brown thinned with water and a no. 0 round to paint the lines.

2. Use thinned Spice Brown on a no. 0 round to paint the basket weave. Let dry. Switch to a no. 14 flat brush sideloaded into Spice Brown, and float a shade next to each basket weave. Let dry.

3. Use a no. 14 flat to float a shade of Spice Brown along the cornucopia top and next to the opening. Sideload the no. 14 flat into Empire Gold and flip-float highlighting in the center of each weave. Let dry. Switch to a no. 0 round loaded into thinned Spice Brown. Pull short uneven lines through the shaded areas to simulate the look of woven straw. Clean the brush and load into thinned Empire Gold. Pull short uneven lines through the highlight areas. Add a line of Empire Gold over the basket weave lines.

4. Add additional Spice Brown shade lines if needed for deepening. Add a touch of Light Ivory to Empire Gold and pull a second highlight over the basket weave down the center of the cornucopia. This helps create the illusion that the cornucopia is rounded. Use a no. 14 flat brush to float a touch of Black on each side of the cornucopia.

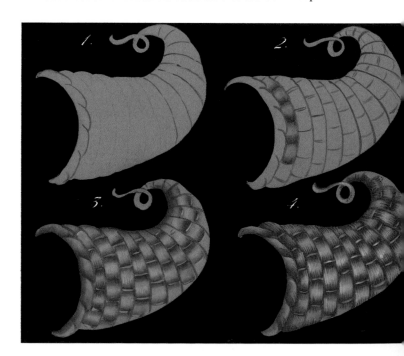

Pineapple & Watermelon

PINEAPPLE

1. Base the pineapple with Spice Brown, using a no. 14 flat brush. Base the leaves with Forest Green and a no. 2 round. Transfer the crosshatch pattern with dark graphite paper. Paint over the graphite lines with thinned Spice Brown on a no. 0 round.

2. Sideload a no. 14 flat brush with Spice Brown. Float a shade on the top and left side of each diamond shape. Load a no. 0 round into Medium Foliage Green and highlight the leaf edges to separate.

3. Deepen the shaded areas of the pineapple diamond shapes with a sideload float of Candy Bar Brown on a no. 14 flat brush. Also float Candy Bar Brown on each side of the pineapple and at the bottom, next to the watermelon. Add a tiny "V" accent on each diamond shape with a no. 0 round loaded into Empire Gold. Pick up Medium Foliage Green on a no. 0 round and pull thin lines from the tips of the leaves, three- quarters of the way down. Add Apple Green to the brush and accent the tip of each leaf.

WATERMELON

1. Base the meat of the watermelon with Red Iron Oxide. Then re-base in Fruit Punch. With a no. 2 round, base the skin with Forest Green and base the rind with Light Ivory.

2. Highlight the middle of the watermelon meat by picking up Fruit Punch on a no. 14 flat, then sideloading a touch of Light Ivory. Blend on the palette before slip-slapping into the middle. You may need to do this step a few times before you get enough highlight. Then side load a no. 14 flat into Candy Bar Brown and shade on the left side and toward the bottom edge of the water-melon meat.

Load a no. 2 round with Medium Foliage Green and add stripes on the skin of the watermelon. Pick up more water and tint the rind with a touch of Medium Foliage Green.

Using a no. 0 round and Black, apply teardrop-shaped seeds in the red area next to the rind.

3. Add dots of Light Ivory on each seed for a highlight. Pick up some Apple Green on a no. 2 round and high-light the stripes on the skin.

Grapes & Apples

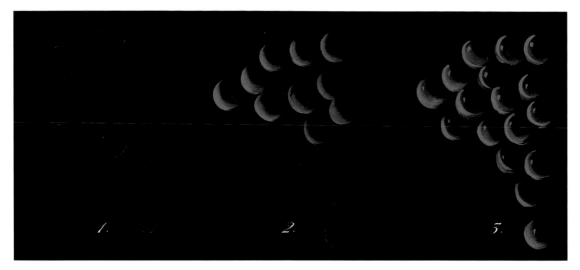

PURPLE GRAPES

1. Base the grapes using a no. 2 round brush and Grape.

2. Sideload a no. 14 flat brush into Vintage Wine and float a shade on the right side of each grape. Using the same brush, sideload into Dusty Plum and float a highlight on the left side of each grape.

3. Load a no. 0 round into Dusty Plum and pull a C-stroke over the highlighted area. Load the same brush into Vintage Wine and pull a C-stroke over the shaded area of each grape. Add a highlight dot of Dusty Plum + Light Ivory (1:1) on the left side of each grape.

GREEN GRAPES

1. Base the green grapes with Apple Green, using a no. 2 round brush.

2. Shade the right side with Medium Foliage Green using a no. 14 flat brush. Highlight the left side using the same brush, side loaded into Light Ivory + Empire Gold (1:1). Add highlight dots of Light Ivory on the left side of each grape.

APPLES

1. Base each apple with Red Iron Oxide. Chalk in or transfer the stem dimple. Paint this dimple with a no. 0 round brush and Candy Bar Brown.

2. Sideload a no. 14 flat brush into Candy Bar Brown. Float a shade under the stem dimple, on the apple's right side and halfway across its bottom edge.

3. Pick up Terra Cotta on a no. 6 filbert and pull highlights through the middle of the apple, down from the shading. Pull a Spice Brown stem, using a no. 0 round.

4. Use the no. 12 Bringle Blender and Empire Gold to stipple a highlight over the Terra Cotta highlight. Follow the same technique you used with the cherries (see page 120, step 3 under "Cherries").

Leaves & Tangerines

LEAVES

1. Base the leaves using a no. 2 round brush and Forest Green. Switch to a no. 0 round to line in the stems.

2. Use a no. 0 round and Medium Foliage Green to pull a vein line in each leaf and to outline the larger leaves.

3. Pull smaller vein lines at an angle from the centerline with the no. 0 round and Medium Foliage Green.

4. Highlight the vein lines and the tips of the leaves with Apple Green, using a no. 0 round. Add highlights to the stem lines as well. Pick up a scant amount of Empire Gold in a no. 12 Bringle Blender brush and stipple an additional highlight at the base of the larger leaves.

TANGERINES

1. Base the tangerines with Terra Cotta. Transfer the pattern line that separates the tangerines and paint over it with a thin amount of Candy Bar Brown on a no. 0 round brush.

2. Sideload a no. 14 flat into Candy Bar Brown and float a shade on the right tangerine to separate the two.

3. Sideload into more Candy Bar Brown and float a shade on the bottom edge of each tangerine.

4. Pick up Empire Gold on a no. 12 Bringle Blender and stipple a highlight in the middle of each tangerine.

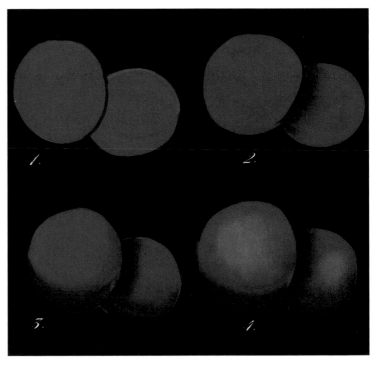

Plums & Strawberries

PLUMS

1. Base the plums with Rhythm 'N Blue. Then separate the plums with a thin line of Vintage Wine. Also line in the indention at the top of each plum.

2. Sideload a no. 14 flat brush with Vintage Wine and float a shade to separate the two plums. Also float a shade on the far right side of the right plum.

3. Float more Vintage Wine on the plum bottoms, using a no. 14 flat.

4. Pick up Dusty Plum on a no. 12 Bringle Blender and stipple a highlight in the middle of each plum. Float more Vintage Wine into the indentations.

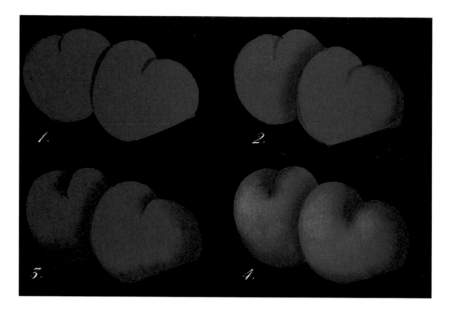

STRAWBERRIES

1. Base the strawberries with Red Iron Oxide. Separate the strawberries with a thin line of Candy Bar Brown.

2. Sideload a no. 14 flat brush with Candy Bar Brown and shade between each strawberry and on the right sides of the lower two.

3. Pick up Empire Gold on a no. 12 Bringle Blender and stipple a highlight in the middle of each strawberry. Base the stem ends and leaves with a no. 0 round brush loaded in Forest Green. Each leaf is a small S-stroke.

4. Base in teardrop-shaped seeds using a no. 0 round loaded in Black. After the seeds are dry, highlight each with a tiny dot of Empire Gold + Light Ivory (1:1). Highlight the stem ends with Apple Green.

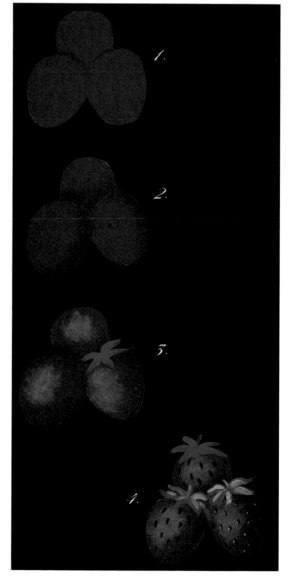

Side of Box, Lid

SIDE OF BOX

Using a 1½-inch (38mm) flat sky wash brush, roughly paint over the box sides with Red Iron Oxide. Let the background show through.

BOX LID SIDE

Hold a ½-inch (13mm) checkerboard stencil over the lid side and stipple Red Iron Oxide into each open square.

Finished Box

Let the box and lid dry completely.

Then erase any leftover pattern lines and apply a protective finish with water-based varnish.

Resources

BRUSHES

Bringle Blender available from
Bette Byrd Brushes
P.O. Box 2526
Duluth, GA 30096
(678) 513-6192
www.bettebyrdbrushes.com

Loew-Cornell
563 Chestnut Avenue
Teaneck, NJ 07666
(201) 836-7070
www.loew-cornell.com

PAINTS & MEDIUMS

DecoArt Inc.
P.O. Box 386
Stanford, KY 40484
800-367-3047
www.decoart.com

Delta Technical Coatings, Inc.
2550 Pellissier Place
Whittier, CA 91601
800-423 4135
www.deltacrafts.com

SURFACES

Pesky Bear
5059 Roszyk Hill Rd.
Machias, NY 14101
716-942-3250
www.peskybear.com

Sechtem's Wood Products
533 Margaret St.
Russell, KS 67665
800-255-4285
www.tolemine.com

Stan Brown's Arts & Crafts
13435 NE Whitaker Way
Portland, OR
800-547-5531
www.stanbrownartsandcrafts.com

Unique Woods
2800 West Division A1
Arlington, TX 76012
800-353-9650
www.uniquewoods.com

Viking Woodcrafts, Inc.
1317 8th Street SE
Waseca, MN 56093
800-328-0116

CANADIAN RETAILERS

Crafts Canada
2745 29th St. N.E.
Calgary, AL T1Y 7B5

Folk Art Enterprises
P.O. Box 1088
Ridgetown, ON, N0P 2C0
Tel: 888-214-0062

MacPherson Craft Wholesale
83 Queen St. E.
P.O. Box 1870
St. Mary's, ON, N4X 1C2
Tel: 519-284-1741

**Maureen McNaughton
Enterprises Inc.**
RR #2
Belwood, ON, N0B 1J0
Tel: 519-843-5648
Fax: 519-843-6022
E-mail:
  maureen.mcnaughton.ent.inc
  @sympatico.ca
www.maureenmcnaughton.com

Mercury Art & Craft Supershop
332 Wellington St.
London, ON, N6C 4P7
Tel: 519-434-1636

**Town & Country
Folk Art Supplies**
93 Green Lane
Thornhill, ON, L3T 6K6
Tel: 905-882-0199

U.K. RETAILERS

Art Express
Design House
Sizers Court
Yeadon LS9 6DP
Tel: 0800 731 4185
www.artexpress.co.uk

Atlantis Art Materials
146 Brick Lane
London E1 6RU
Tel: 020 7377 8855

Crafts World (head office)
No. 8 North Street, Guildford
Surrey GU1 4AF
Tel: 07000 757070

Green & Stone
259 King's Road
London SW3 5EL
Tel: 020 7352 0837
E-mail:
  greenandstone@enterprise.net

Hobby Crafts (head office)
River Court
Southern Sector
Bournemouth International Airport
Christchurch
Dorset BH23 6SE
Tel: 0800 272387

Homecrafts Direct
P.O. Box 38
Leicester LE1 9BU
Tel: 0116 251 3139

Index

The best in decorative painting instruction and inspiration is from North Light Books!

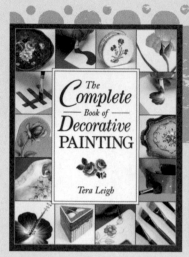

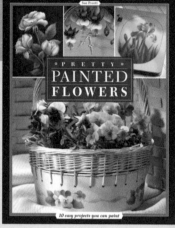

This book is the must-have, one-stop reference for decorative painters, crafters, home decorators and do-it-yourselfers. It's packed with solutions to every painting challenge, including surface preparation, lettering, borders, faux finishes, stroke-work techniques and more! You'll also find five fun-to-paint projects designed to instruct, challenge and entertain you—no matter what your skill level.

ISBN 1-58180-062-2, paperback, 256 pages, #31803-K

Fill your home with the time-less charm of folk art scenes! Popular instructors Judy Diep-house and Lynne Deptula team up to show you how to capture the quaint and picturesque beau-ty of rolling farmland, old-fash-ioned barns, churches and country gardens. You'll find ten projects for adorning every-thing from wooden boxes and mitten chests to picnic baskets and lamp shades. Easy-to-trace patterns, paint color charts and start-to-finish instructions make each project a joy to create.

ISBN 1-58180-117-3, paperback, 128 pages, #31813-K

Create beautiful floral paintings with exquisite detail from petal to stem. From dusty pink roses to dramatic hydrangeas and dain-ty lily-of-the-valley, you'll find step-by-step instruction for paint-ing your favorite florals on a variety of surfaces. Each stun-ning project includes a complete supply list, easy to follow work-sheets and patterns.

ISBN 1-58180-461-X, paperback, 48 pages, #32718-K

Learn to paint still life objects that look so real you can almost reach out and touch them! Mary McLean, master of realistic painting, shares her unique approach for dramatic results. You'll find projects for all skill levels including old-time crock-ery, glass jelly jars, colorful enamelware, tulips, daffodils, roses, shiny red apples and more on a variety of surfaces.

ISBN 1-58180-299-4, paperback, 128 pages, #32235-K

These books and other fine North Light titles are available from your local art & craft retailer, bookstore, online supplier or by calling 1-800-448-0915.